EBBSFLEET
UNITED

FORMATIVE YEARS

GRAVESEND UNITED

1893 – Club formed by merger of Gravesend FC
and Gravesend Ormonde

	P.	W.	D.	L.	F.	A.	Pts	Pos.
KENT LEAGUE – Division 1								
1893–94	16	6	5	5	54	33	17	4th
1894–95	22	10	4	8	36	45	20	7th
1895–96	19	1	2	16	23	81	4	11th
SOUTHERN LEAGUE – Division 1								
1896–97	20	9	4	7	35	34	22	5th
1897–98	22	7	6	9	28	39	20	8th
1898–99	24	7	5	12	42	52	19	11th
1899–00	28	10	4	14	38	58	24	12th
1900–01	28	6	7	15	32	85	19	13th

Rejoined KENT LEAGUE for one season before
playing succession of local friendlies

	P.	W.	D.	L.	F.	A.	Pts	Pos.
KENT LEAGUE – Division 1								
1905–06	14	10	1	3	44	21	21	2nd
1906–07	14	7	1	6	42	24	15	3rd
1907–08	14	5	1	8	21	26	11	7th
1908–09	16	11	3	2	40	16	25	2nd
1909–10	22	9	5	8	34	36	23	6th
1910–11	26	8	6	12	37	53	22	7th
1911–12	28	12	5	11	64	50	29	5th
1912–13	28	7	7	14	34	52	21	12th
1913–14	30	10	6	14	50	57	26	11th

Suspended due to war – did not reform until
1932 after losing their ground

	P.	W.	D.	L.	F.	A.	Pts	Pos.
KENT AMATEUR LEAGUE – Division 1								
1932–33	14	8	2	4	38	26	18	2nd
KENT LEAGUE – Division 2								
1933–34	24	13	4	7	75	46	30	4th
1934–35	24	8	1	15	46	100	17	10th
KENT AMATEUR LEAGUE – Western Section								
1935–36	20	16	3	1	86	32	35	1st
1936–37	20	10	3	7	41	38	23	5th
1937–38	20	12	4	4	46	24	28	3rd
1938–39	24	6	6	12	53	92	18	8th

Suspended due to war

	P.	W.	D.	L.	F.	A.	Pts	Pos.
KENT LEAGUE								
1944–45	18	7	3	8	28	37	17	7th
1945–46	20	9	3	8	42	23	21	3rd

NORTHFLEET UNITED

1890 – Club formed

	P.	W.	D.	L.	F.	A.	Pts	Pos.
KENT LEAGUE – Division 1								
1895–96	22	16	2	4	85	31	34	1st
SOUTHERN LEAGUE – Division 1								
1896–97	20	5	4	11	24	46	14	9th
1897–98	22	4	3	15	29	60	11	11th
Rejoined KENT LEAGUE but withdrew after 7 matches –	7	3	2	2	26	19	8	8th
WEST KENT LEAGUE								
1903–04	12	1	3	8	10	31	5	7th
1904–05	20	7	3	10	37	50	17	8th
1905–06	16	7	2	7	23	26	16	5th
KENT LEAGUE – Division 1								
1906–07	14	10	0	4	39	17	20	2nd
1907–08	16	14	1	1	54	13	29	1st
1908–09	16	13	1	2	51	23	27	1st
1909–10	22	17	2	3	74	31	36	1st
1910–11	26	7	4	15	38	64	18	13th
1911–12	28	10	5	13	47	48	25	8th
1912–13	28	14	5	9	58	55	33	4th
1913–14	30	17	5	8	63	49	37	4th
Suspended due to war								
1919–20	24	19	3	2	70	22	41	1st
1920–21	32	21	3	8	76	40	45	3rd
1921–22	28	18	6	4	78	36	42	2nd
1922–23	32	17	5	10	88	41	39	4th
1923–24	30	15	5	10	61	35	35	4th
1924–25	34	29	1	4	114	25	59	2nd
1925–26	36	29	3	4	172	48	61	1st
1926–27	26	15	3	8	79	51	33	5th
SOUTHERN LEAGUE – Eastern Section								
1927–28	34	17	7	10	83	54	41	3rd
1928–29	36	17	4	15	87	65	38	9th
1929–30	32	6	7	19	53	77	19	16th
KENT LEAGUE – Division 1								
1930–31	36	21	3	12	124	59	45	5th
1931–32	36	32	2	2	138	22	66	1st
1932–33	34	28	1	5	126	50	57	2nd
1933–34	36	23	2	11	122	47	48	4th
1934–35	36	26	7	3	110	30	59	1st
1935–36	36	26	5	5	158	41	57	1st
1936–37	32	25	2	5	128	29	52	1st
1937–38	32	23	5	4	116	29	51	3rd
1938–39	28	20	4	4	125	38	44	1st

Suspended due to war – did not reform

GRAVESEND & NORTHFLEET

Ebbsfleet United

PAUL HARRISON

The History Press

First published 2012

The History Press
The Mill, Brimscombe Port
Stroud, Gloucestershire, GL5 2QG
www.thehistorypress.co.uk

British Library Cataloguing in Publication Data.
A catalogue record for this book is available from the British Library.

ISBN 978 0 7524 6409 1

Typesetting and origination by The History Press
Printed in Great Britain

CONTENTS

ABOUT THE AUTHOR

Paul Harrison was born in Gravesend in 1948 and has lived in the area all his life. Educated at Dover Road Primary and Northfleet Secondary Modern Schools, he began following the club in 1955 as a seven-year-old in the company of his father and has followed them through thick and thin ever since.

Although preferring to stay in the background these days he was programme editor between 1982 and 1990 and a member of the Supporters' Association committee for twenty years, holding most of the positions of office between 1981 and 2000 when he relinquished all roles within the club except his contribution to the programme with historical articles.

He is particularly proud of his unique hat-trick of achievements within the club between 1988 and 1990 when he was programme editor, away coach driver and turnstile operator. He is these days a season ticket holder and member of both myfc and Fleet Trust.

This is his seventh book following *Southern League Post War Years* (1987), *Southern League The First Fifty Years* (1990), *Cup Glory* (1995), *Gravesend & Northfleet Golden Jubilee* (1996), *Images of Sport: Gravesend & Northfleet FC* (2006) and *FA Cup Giantkillers* (2007).

The author (he's the one on the right) discusses the Fleet's prospects with his new best friend on the Rock of Gibraltar September 2011.

INTRODUCTION

Much has changed since *Images of Sport: Gravesend & Northfleet FC* was published in 2006 to celebrate the club's diamond jubilee – not least a name change to Ebbsfleet United. Stir into the mix a takeover by the first ever internet-owned club – myfootballclub, with a peak of 36,000 members – a triumphant first ever appearance at Wembley Stadium, relegation and then instant promotion, plans for a new ground dashed and a serious downturn in the economy leaving the thousands of houses intended for the Ebbsfleet area unbuilt – losing many of the potential supporters expected – and you have a series of events that need more than the originally intended minor update to the book. With this in mind it was decided to produce a 50/50 selection of old and new material particularly concentrating on Ebbsfleet United, but not forgetting the all-important roots of the club.

Six years ago when the original book was written, things were already on the move with Fleet Social Club – the former sports club of Bowater Scott (Kimberly Clark) – being put into the care of the club by Gravesham Council for use by the club for training and to involve the local population in both sporting and social activities. The idea was to bring in profits to try to help the club's decision to go full time and step up to the tough challenge of Conference football and the much larger clubs the team were now competing against. Another prospect of boosting finances came with the opening of Ebbsfleet International railway station just a drop kick away from the ground. A lucrative sponsorship with Eurostar, a record for non-league football, was arranged but it required a name change to Ebbsfleet United; this did not go down well with supporters especially as there was no vote to decide this, but with the financial situation getting more serious by the day there really was no alternative and although nearly everyone was sad to lose the traditional name, it was soon begrudgingly accepted. This was followed by an even more sensational event when the fledgling myfootballclub – an entirely new concept for fanpower – decided to opt for a majority share in the club after previously being linked with clubs such as Leeds United and Nottingham Forest. Although many were disappointed with the selection of Ebbsfleet as the team, it did not stop the membership of myfc rising to well over 30,000 and many were rewarded by a trip to Wembley to see their newly adopted club beat Torquay United in front of a 40,000 crowd. This memorable achievement should have been lift-off time for the club but instead proved the high water mark. Money was wasted by ill-conceived and extravagant ideas and disillusion soon set in among myfc members who having stumped up £35 to join failed to renew after one year, with plummeting membership resulting in a serious shortfall in anticipated revenue.

By the start of 2009/10 all but a couple of contracted players had been released and a new team had to be built from scratch on a shoestring with the inevitable relegation following. Another bodyblow had also been received with the hopeful new ground being vetoed as unsuitable and a cycling complex being built instead. As a consolation though, the local council saved the historic Stonebridge Road ground, buying it before it came up for auction and all the uncertainty this would have produced with no guarantee football would be continued.

Yet another fly in the ointment was that the club were no longer training at Fleet Social, deeming it unsuitable and at present legal discussions are ongoing on this subject. At least the story ends on a happy note, the club winning promotion in the Blue Square South play-offs back to the national division, this being achieved on a dramatic and sunny afternoon in Farnborough where a crowd of 4,000-plus was made up of a huge Fleet following of more than 2,000 who showed once again a winning team would get support.

Paul Harrison, 2012

1

IN THE BEGINNING
1890–1922

Northfleet Invicta, as they were originally known, played their first game on the Wombwell
Hall estate on a site close to the Six Bells (pictured) in Old Perry Street on 8 November 1890.
The side had been established in the year as a cricket team and turned its attention to football
as autumn began. Nearly all teenagers, they played friendly matches – although the term
was only a loose description as the games were described as crude affairs allowing hacking,
scrimmaging, barging and occasionally punching. With no referees at any matches other
than the top ones, the teams had to adjudicate all the decisions between themselves – which
of course led to further arguments.

Gravesend United were formed in 1893 by a merger between Gravesend Ormonde who played at the Bat and Ball ground and Gravesend who played at Fairfields on the Overcliffe on a site behind what is now the Overcliffe Hotel (pictured) and bordered by St James Avenue and Lennox Avenue. The Shrimpers then became founder members of the Kent League in 1893/94 and moved on to their next ground in Pelham Road, now occupied by Gravesend Grammar School for Girls, a site the club lost in 1914 when it was requisitioned by the War Office before going to Kent CC. Although they were offered a ground share with Northfleet United they declined and did not play another game until 1932 – eighteen years after their previous match!

With football gradually becoming more organised Northfleet entered the Kent League for the first time in 1895/96 and won the championship at the first time of asking. Here, the team pose in traditional Victorian style with the trophy. The fourteen-man squad comprised Bundock (captain), Walker, King, Auld, Wright, Cullen, Ware, Grieves, Russell, Ferguson, Moody, McGregor, Hills and Cottam. Following this success it was time to move on, to Portland Meadows (now the huge Northfleet Cement Works) and then Huntley Meadows (now Huntley Avenue) where the ground ran parallel with the main railway line to London.

1897-98

First Division

	P	W	D	L	F	A	Pts
Southampton	22	18	1	3	53	18	37
Bristol City	22	13	7	2	67	33	33
Tottenham Hotspur	22	12	4	6	52	31	28
Chatham	22	12	4	6	50	34	28
Reading	22	8	7	7	39	31	23
New Brompton	22	9	4	9	37	37	22
Sheppey United	22	10	1	11	40	49	21
Gravesend United	22	7	6	9	28	39	20
Millwall Athletic	22	8	2	12	48	45	18
Swindon Town	22	7	2	13	36	48	16
Northfleet	22	4	3	15	29	60	11
Wolverton L & NW Railway	22	3	1	18	28	82	7

1900-01

First Division

	P	W	D	L	F	A	Pts
Southampton	28	18	5	5	58	26	41
Bristol City	28	17	5	6	54	27	39
Portsmouth	28	17	4	7	56	32	38
Millwall Athletic	28	17	2	9	55	32	36
Tottenham Hotspur	28	16	4	8	55	33	36
West Ham United	28	14	5	9	40	28	33
Bristol Rovers	28	14	4	10	46	35	32
Queens Park Rangers	28	11	4	13	43	48	26
Reading	28	8	8	12	24	25	24
Luton Town	28	11	2	15	43	49	24
Kettering	28	7	9	12	33	46	23
New Brompton	28	7	5	16	34	51	19
Gravesend United	28	6	7	15	32	85	19
Watford	28	6	4	18	24	52	16
Swindon Town	28	3	8	17	19	47	14

These two tables from the Southern League show how, at the dawn of the twentieth century, the local clubs were mixing with the elite of southern England. This was the time when a combined team would have been strong enough to challenge the best and would probably have been strong enough for a Football League place. It is worth noting that in 1900/01, when Tottenham famously became the first and last non-league team to win the FA Cup, Gravesend beat them 2–1 at Pelham Road in the league, although they suffered a 5–1 defeat at White Hart Lane.

An 1890 view of Stonebridge Road with the Plough public house and behind it the grand-looking Huggens College – a home for old folk demolished in the late 1960s and replaced by flats. In the foreground is Plough pond. If the camera had panned 90 degrees to the left where the ground now stands, water meadows would be seen all the way down to the River Thames 600 yards away. The cement company APCM (later Blue Circle) owned huge tracts of land and would provide the ground for the football club at a peppercorn rent fifteen years later because so many local people worked for them; it helped to develop good relations with the people. It was Northfleet's fourth and final ground and the first game was played on 2 September 1905 against East Ham in a friendly which Northfleet won 1–0. It would become one of the best and largest grounds in non-league football before its sad decline in the late twentieth century.

Gravesend United line up at their Pelham Road ground before taking on local rivals Northfleet United. The date is 18 March 1905 and the Shrimpers beat the Fleet (or Cementers, as they were also often called) 2–0 in a West Kent League game in front of a crowd of 3,000. Back row, left to right: H. Porter, C. Stapley, S. Parkinson, F. Obee, T. Penney, referee, R. Colquhoun. Front row: J. Seppitt, H. Mann, E. Parkinson, Sir Gilbert Parker MP, E. Mann, L. Stott, T. Smith.

GRAVESEND UNITED FOOTBALL CLUB.

GROUND:
Sports Ground, Pelham Road.

HEADQUARTERS:
15 Milton Road, Gravesend.

Dear Sir,

You are selected to play for the above Club on *Saturday*

next, the *23rd* day of *September* 190*5*, against

Maidstone United / Thames & Medway Combination at *Maidstone*   Kick-off *3.30* sharp.

Yours truly,

J. D. Seppit

The Train leaves *Gravesend Central* Station at *2.18* sharp.

A postcard for Gravesend forward Len Stott informing him of his selection for the match at Maidstone on 23 September 1905. Len lived in Toronto Road, Tilbury, so would have caught the Tilbury–Gravesend ferry (then a very frequent service and the only means of getting from Essex to Kent without going via London). After disembarking he would have presumably strolled up Gravesend High Street and Windmill Street and met his team-mates at what was then Gravesend Central station.

Jimmy Ashcroft (1870–1940). Born in Bootle, he moved from the Merseyside area where his goalkeeping career was going nowhere and found himself in Gravesend where he signed for the Shrimpers in time for the 1898/99 Southern League season where he became an instant success helping them win the Kent Senior Cup. His performances had been noted by the only Football League club in the south of England – Woolwich Arsenal – who signed him after that single successful season with the Shrimpers. It was a wise move as Jimmy continued his improvement and became the first Arsenal player to appear for England, winning three caps in 1905/6 and keeping two clean sheets. He moved on to Blackburn Rovers in 1908 and was there when they became Football League champions in 1913 before ending his career where it had started on Merseyside, this time with Tranmere Rovers.

Charles Buchan (1891–1960), one of the legends of the first half of the twentieth century. Born in Plumstead, his career appeared to be going nowhere at Woolwich Arsenal and he signed for Northfleet in 1909 where he made an immediate impact, helping the club to a hat-trick of trophies in his only season. Charles moved to Leyton and then on to Sunderland where he played from 1910 to 1924, making 380 appearances and scoring 209 goals. He won a League title and an FA Cup runners-up medal there and is still revered in the area as one of their all-time greats. He moved back down south to play for Arsenal between 1924 and 1927 and although by now a veteran he still scored 49 goals in 102 games, gaining a second FA Cup runners-up medal. The England international retired after this to enjoy a second successful career as a sports journalist, first with the *News Chronicle* and then founding his own football magazine in 1951, the *Charles Buchan Football Monthly*. He died in the South of France in 1961.

Harry Howell (1890–1932). Harry was one of several footballer/cricketers to play for Northfleet United at a time when the two games didn't overlap in the way they do now. Harry was a regular with Warwickshire and played five times for England as a fast bowler while playing as a half-back for Wolves and Accrington Stanley. He moved to Northfleet playing at Stonebridge Road in the 1921/22 season.

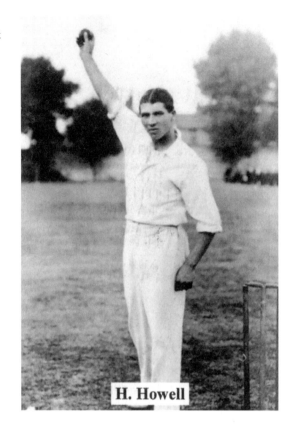

H. Howell

Bill Jacques (1888–1925). Northfleet-born Bill was the first outstanding player produced by Northfleet United. A fine goalkeeper, he moved to Coventry City in 1911 after helping the Fleet win both the Kent League and Kent Senior Cup. He then moved onto Tottenham where he was ever-present in the side that won the Second Division Championship in 1919/20 but missed out on their 1921 FA Cup triumph through injury. His poor health forced his retirement in 1923 after amassing 238 appearances for Spurs and he sadly died at Dartford in 1925 aged only thirty-six.

Northfleet United produced their greatest team yet in 1909/10, completing a hat-trick of Kent League titles and a treble for the season by adding the Kent Senior Cup and the Thames and Medway Combination. Unfortunately, by the time this celebration photo was taken two key players – inside forward Charles Buchan and goalkeeper Bill Jacques – had moved on. Back row (players only), left to right: Rogers, Fox, Quail. Middle row: Crowhurst, Williams, Kennedy, Jeacock, Hams. Front row: Nash, Myers, Sharpe. Sadly, both Kennedy and Myers were killed during the First World War.

Northfleet United recorded a fifth Kent League title in 1919/20. Back row (players only), left to right: Evans, Seccombe, Good, Green, Gegus, Lawrence, Makepiece, Harbor. Front row: Daisley, Jewhurst, Tyler (captain).

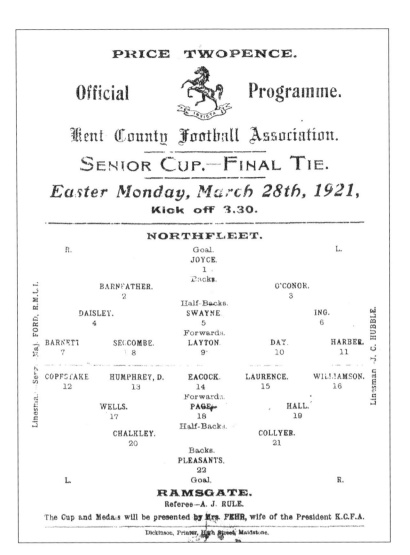

PRICE TWOPENCE.

Official Programme.

Kent County Football Association.

SENIOR CUP.—FINAL TIE.

Easter Monday, March 28th, 1921,
Kick off 3.30.

NORTHFLEET.

R.   Goal.   L.
JOYCE.
1
Backs.
BARNFATHER.   O'CONOR.
2   3
Half-Backs.
DAISLEY.   SWAYNE.   ING.
4   5   6
Forwards.
BARNETT   SECCOMBE.   LAYTON.   DAY.   HARBER.
7   8   9   10   11

COPESTAKE   HUMPHREY, D.   EACOCK.   LAURENCE.   WILLIAMSON.
12   13   14   15   16
Forwards.
WELLS.   PAGE.   HALL.
17   18   19
Half-Backs.
CHALKLEY.   COLLYER.
20   21
Backs.
PLEASANTS.
23
L.   Goal.   R.

RAMSGATE.
Referee—A. J. RULE.

The Cup and Medals will be presented by Mrs. FEHR, wife of the President K.C.F.A.

Dickinson, Printer, High Street, Maidstone.

Above left: A large crowd, estimated at more than 10,000, packed into Maidstone to see Northfleet overcome Ramsgate 1–0, a seventieth-minute Arthur Seccombe goal deciding the issue and giving the Fleet a fourth Kent Senior Cup triumph.

Above right: Arthur Seccombe, a real Fleet legend. From the time he joined the club from local football as an eighteen-year-old in 1911 until his retirement in 1926 as a thirty-three-year-old he played more games (450) and scored more goals (250) than any other player. His medal collection, comprising a record six Kent Senior Cups, two Kent League Championships and one Kent League Cup, highlighted a brillant career.

The Northfleet end of Stonebridge Road is packed to see the home side beat Sheppey United 4–1 in the first qualifying round of the FA Cup on 9 October 1920. Fleet went on to beat Worthing 5–0 in the next round before exiting at Maidstone by the same scoreline. Apart from minor improvements, the Northfleet end would remain the same until the early 1950s when a large covered terrace was built – one of the largest stands in non-league football. Sadly, the years took their toll, culminating in the stand's closure by the safety authorities in 2005. Seating was installed in 2006.

2

THE TOTTENHAM
CONNECTION
1923–45

Stonebridge Road in 1932, when the main stand was still in its full glory. On the Stonebridge Road side of the ground is the small stand rescued from the ailing Rosherville Gardens, complete with ornate pillaring, which stood on the ground from 1909 until it was dismantled in 1953. Both goal sides look pretty basic, although there was some terracing. But one thing never changes, as the groundsman can be seen on the pitch, grafting away.

Billy Lane

Bill Lane (1904–85). In 1923 an historic agreement was made between Northfleet and Tottenham Hotspur, providing the Fleet with a batch of promising Spurs youngsters each season to help knock off their rough edges and give them vital experience in the tough world of non-league football. Bill Lane was in the first intake of 1923/24 and had a memorable single season; although only fourth place was attained in the league, the club swept to victory in the Kent Senior Cup and Kent League Cup, while a draw with Gillingham earned them a half-share in the Kent Senior Shield. The centre forward was never able to pin down a regular place in the Spurs side and went on to have successful spells at Watford, Brentford and Bristol City. After the Second World War he moved into management with good results at both Guildford and Brighton. In 1961 he came full circle and ended up back where it had all started for him at Stonebridge Road. He was in charge during the legendary FA Cup run of 1962/63 but the club's league form was desperately disappointing, ending in relegation, and Bill resigned at the end of that season.

Albert Ringrose

Bert Ringrose (1916–68). Edmonton-born Bert achieved a unique record by being the only player to perform for Northfleet United (1934–6), Tottenham Hotspur (1937–9) and Gravesend & Northfleet (1946–7). An accomplished full-back, he played in the very first game for the newly formed Gravesend & Northfleet in 1946.

Between 1924 and 1928, Northfleet United won the Kent Senior Cup a record five times in succession, a record that still stands today. These were the days of 10,000-strong crowds for the final, when all Kent stopped and the winning side were given civic receptions by the grateful home borough. The victories were achieved against Dartford 1–0, Sittingbourne 8–2, Folkstone 1–0, Sheppey 1–0 and Sittingbourne 3–1. Two players, forwards Bell and Pilcher, played in all five finals.

1924
Northfleet's Cup of Joy.
FINAL DAY AT MAIDSTONE.
Dartford Beaten in a Moderate Game

1925
NORTHFLEET RETAIN KENT SENIOR CUP
REMARKABLE FOOTBALL AGAINST SITTINGBOURNE

EIGHT GOALS FOR TWO AGAINST

1926
NARROW VICTORY OVER FOLKESTONE

NORTHFLEET WIN THE CUP
1927
How Northfleet Won the Cup.
Holders for Four Successive Years

CAPITAL GAME AGAINST SHEPPEY

1928
KENT SENIOR CUP
Northfleet Win Trophy for Fifth Successive Year

BLUNDERS BY SITTINGBOURNE GOALKEEPER

KENT SENIOR CUP

Northfleet Win Trophy for Fifth Successive Year

BLUNDERS BY SITTINGBOURNE GOALKEEPER

Northfleet United Football Club improved upon their own Kent Senior Cup record on Easter Monday, when, by defeating Sittingbourne by 3—1, they won the Blue Riband of Kent football for the fifth successive season.

That Northfleet won on their merits was generally agreed. It was a game fully typical of cup football, science for the most part going by the board in favour of robust kick-and-rush methods. Both teams have given better displays this season in far smaller "gates." But the Cup was the thing, and the thousands of spectators were treated to ninety minutes of end-to-end football with the ultimate issue in doubt till near the end. Here is a tabloid timetable of the match:—

3.31: Game commenced.
3.38: North scored for Northfleet.
4.15: Cox equalised (penalty).
4.16: End of first half.
4.20: Second half began.
4.42: Bell put Northfleet ahead.
4.48: Edmonds increased lead.
5.13: Match finished.
5.30: Presentation ceremony.

The great trek to Maidstone Athletic Ground—the scene of so many of Northfleet's former triumphs—began before midday. Dull skies did not deter enthusiasts and there were animated scenes all along the route from this district to the County Town. More motor-cars were on the road than at any previous Easter Monday, and the hundreds of private cars were augmented by quite a fleet of motor coaches. Many commercial vehicles were also pressed into service. Hundreds of supporters of both teams went on motor-cycles and push-bikes, and the new prehistoric horse and trap was not entirely absent.

THREE SPECIAL TRAINS

from Northfleet and Gravesend were very well filled. About nine o'clock the sun broke through and an azure sky displaced the leaden clouds of the forenoon. Hawkers of rosettes (red and white for Northfleet's "fans," red and blue for the supporters of Sittingbourne) did brisk business. Inside the Athletic Ground the scene, viewed from the stand was a memorable one, the firm smooth turf being encircled by thousands eager for the annual struggle to begin. As the hour for the kick-off approached the stands and enclosures rapidly filled, and when Chaplin led Northfleet out to a roar of cheering there was only standing room in its reserved parts of the enclosure. A minute later another big shout greeted Dickie and his men, resplendent in new black and red shirts and black shorts. In the main stand were prominent personages in the sporting and social life of Kent, among them Mr. Frank Fehr, C.B.E. (President of the K.C.F.A.) and Mrs. and Miss Fehr, Mr. Irving J. Albery, M.P., Mrs. Albery, and prominent officials of the County Football Association, among them Major R. A. Porter, J.P., Mr. J. B. Longho, J.P., and Mr. S. J. W. Brown (Secretary).

Both sides were at full strength, Northfleet being represented by the team that defeated Sheppey on Good Friday, Sittingbourne made an eleventh hour change, Kirby the regular outside-right coming in for S. Wiles.

Teams and officials:—
Northfleet: Cummings; Illingworth, Chaplin; Rowe, Pye Houston; Pilcher, North, Edmonds, Bell, Alford.
Sittingbourne: Bailey; E. M. Batchelor, Regan; V. H. Jones, Dickie, Newton; Kirby, Gilgun, H. Wiles, Burgess and Cox.
Referee: Mr. J. G. Woodley.
Linesmen: Mr. W. F. Wenborn and A. W. Twyman.

THE PLAY.

Chaplin won the toss from Dickie and thereby enabled Northfleet to have the stiffish breeze and sun at their backs. Sittingbourne had to defend the Orchard end. There was plenty of pace and vigour at the start, and within a minute Batchelor grassed Alford, who was cutting along with a fine pass from Houston. The latter placed the resultant free-kick wide. Next minute Cox threatened until Rowe neatly robbed him. Then came a test for Cummings—one of the few good shots of the match. Cox was the marksman with a finely-placed effort that Northfleet's goalkeeper tipped over the woodwork. The corner hit the side net. Sittingbourne had the territorial advantage for a while until Pye dashed into the fray and broke up a bout of passing. Play after this was concentrated on the Fleets' left for some time and the ball was frequently in touch. A couple of really fine clearances by Chaplin were followed by the first goal. This came in the seventh minute and was in the nature of a gift. Edmonds commenced the movement, working out to the left of the goal before tapping the ball across to North. The last-named sent in a low, slow shot that should not have caused Bailey any bother. Instead, he fumbled the ball and it rolled over the line. Mr. Wordley promptly awarded a goal, though the Sittingbourne players stoutly protested.

The game was fought out at a great pace after this and each side had a share in the exchanges. Jones was injured in a hot attack, but resumed after attention. A foul by Gilgun on Houston enabled the Reds to advance again, but the effort petered out when Houston shot well wide from long range. Within a minute Northfleet renewed the offensive and this time Alford cleverly diddled Jones before accurately middling the ball. In the melee that ensued Bailey rushed from his goal and lost the leather to Pilcher. A corner was conceded and cleared.

FEARLESS TACKLING

Rowe and Houston figured prominently in the following play and it was largely due to their fearless tackling and spoiling that Cox and Kirby were so often subdued. Dickie, too, was getting through a great deal of work. One of his long passes met the right wing moving quickly, and although Kirby squared the ball nicely the Northfleet defence cleared with ease. A counter attack followed at once and this time North displayed smart footwork in partnership with Pilcher. The little winger sported a clear course and shot obliquely. Dickie saved the effort and a few seconds later Jones charged down a fast ground drive by Alford. Sterling back play on the part of Regan was the next feature. Northfleet gained the ascendancy now by dint of speedy and smart short-passing, and one swift move by Bell and Edmonds placed Alford in possession again. However, his fast header was off the target. When the Brickies replied Cox was robbed by Rowe and the ball rolled over the touch-line. A spectator made a lunge at it, but his balance and equipoise. The spectators roared their appreciation of the diversion. There was some hefty first-time kicking by Illingworth and Batchelor before the slackhaired Dickie saved with a mountainous "boot" from Pilcher's centre. Offside against Alford enabled the Black and Red to progress once more and this time Burgess severely tested Cummings, who went down and effected a spectacular save. Houston caught the eye after this and his pass enabled Alford to set out on another touchline journey. The resultant middle was got away by Dickie.

A record fifth successive Kent Senior Cup victory was recorded on Easter Monday 1928 with a 3–1 victory over Sittingbourne.

George Ludford (1915–2001). The free-scoring Barnet-born centre forward became a goalscoring legend in his three years at Stonebridge Road (1933–6). Only 10st in weight and 5ft 6in tall, he needed to be fleet of foot against the bruising Kent League defenders he came up against and the fact he blitzed an amazing 104 league and cup goals in 1935/36 showed just how effective he was. He won two Kent League titles and a Kent League Cup winners' medal before returning to Spurs, where he was never able to really nail down a regular place, making 75 appearances in a long spell at White Hart Lane that spanned the Second World War. He later managed and became a director at Enfield.

Bill Nicholson

The Tottenham Hotspur link-up through the 1920s and '30s enabled supporters to see some future legends take their first steps on the way to fame while in the red colours of Northfleet. Among them was Bill Nicholson (1919–2004) probably the most famous and revered of all their legends. Born in Scarborough, Nicholson was a Fleet player between 1936 and 1938, winning his first senior honour here before winning titles as both player and manager for Spurs. However, he earned just one cap for England.

Ron Burgess (1917–2005). The Welsh-born future captain of Spurs and Wales led his team to successive Second and First Division titles between 1949 and 1951. As he frequently admitted, he was toughened up by his two years of non-league football at Stonebridge Road. He was capped 32 times for Wales.

Ron Burgess

Ted Ditchburn

Ted Ditchburn (1921–2005). Gillingham-born Ted moved to Northfleet as a schoolboy and after giving up the idea of following his dad into the boxing ring, played for Northfleet and signed terms for Spurs in 1938 becoming the final player from the Northfleet production line to leave Spurs in 1958. He was capped 6 times for England.

Gravesend United finally emerged from their long slumber in 1932 after losing their Pelham Road ground to the War Ministry during the First World War. After several false starts they began playing at Central Avenue and are pictured here during the 1932/33 season when they were members of the Kent Amateur League.

IPSWICH TOWN

*Colours—***Blue and White.**

Kick-off **3.0** *p.m.*

1—HOULDSWORTH
Goalkeeper.

2—SHUFFLEBOTTOM
Right Back.

3—PARRY
Left Back.

4—COWIE
Right Half.

5—BURNS
Centre Half.

6—McLUCKIE
Left Half.

7—MURANEY
Outside Right

8—CARTER
Inside Right.

9.—EDWARDS
Centre Forward.

10—J. LITTLE
Inside Left.

11 HAYS
Outside Left.

Referee—A. Grundy (Gt. Bealings).

Linesmen : V. J. Palfrey (Ipswich)
Red flag
A. O. Grant (Shotley)
Blue Flag

12.—W. ADAM or (D. REVELL)
Outside Left.

13.—D. COULSTON
Inside Left.

14.—TRAILOR
Centre Forward

15.—SKINNER
Inside Right.

16—F. COX
Outside Right

17.—R. BURGESS
Left Half.

18.— SMITH
Centre Half.

19.—HISCOKE
Right Half.

20.—W. NICHOLSON
Left Back.

21.—ROBERTS
Right Back.

22.—BARRON
Goalkeeper.

NORTHFLEET UNITED

Colours —Red.

Ipswich Town v Northfleet United in 1937 at a time the Suffolk club were on the rise and a four-course meal cost only 1*s* 9*d*.

Northfleet United line up in 1936/37, the season they were destined to take the Kent League title for the tenth time overall and the third in a row. Back row, left to right: S. Levett (hon. secretary), W.J. Treadwell (vice-chairman), A. Smith, L. Hiscoke, H. Leonard, G. Barron, R. Burgess, J. Roberts, C. Revell, J. Lingham (president), W.H. Hardy (chairman). Front row: J. Anderson (trainer), F. Cox, G. Skinner, J. Coxford, C. Trailor, D. Coulston, A. Day.

A first taste of success for future stars Bill Nicholson and Ron Burgess as they celebrate a hard-fought 1938 Kent Senior Cup final victory, 2–1 against Dover. Sadly it was to be the tenth and last time the club won the competition. Back row (players only), left to right: Nicholson, Revell, Barron, Coxford (with cup), Skinner, Trailor, Burgess, Evans. Front row: Coulston, Day, Roberts.

TOTTENHAM HOTSPUR PLAYERS WHO MADE FOOTBALL LEAGUE APPEARANCES(IN BRACKETS) AND THEIR NORTHFLEET UNITED CAREER SPANS.

Joe Allen (1)   1932-34
Wally Alsford (81) 1929-30
Les Bennett (272) 1938-39
Vic Buckingham (204) 1934-35
Ron Burgess (297) 1936-38
Fred Channell (95) 1932-33
Freddie Cox (99) 1936-38
Alf Day (13)   1928-31
Ted Ditchburn (418) 1938-39
Bill Edrich (20)   1934-35
Albert Evans (5) 1926-27
Arthur Hitchins (35) 1934-36
Percy Hooper (97) 1933-35
Les Howe (165)   1928-32
Doug Hunt (17)   1932-34
Jack Illingworth (10)   1927-29
Charles Jones (18)   1932-34
Eddie King (1)   1933-34
Billy Lane (26)   1923-24

David Levane (8)   1931-32
George Ludford (75)   1933-36
Les Medley (150)   1937-39
Johny Morrison (133)   1931-32
Bill Nicholson (314)   1936-38
Taffy O'Callaghan (252)   1925-27
Ernie Phypers (30)   1933-34
Jack Richardson (38)   1924-25
Bert Ringrose (10)   1934-36
Tommy Roe (7)   1924-25
Arthur Rowe (182)   1925-29
Arthur Sanders (13)   1923-30
Fred Sargent (93)   1934-35
George Skinner (1)   1937-39
Harry Skit (212)   1923-24
Sid Tickridge (95)   1939-40
Cyril Trailor (11)   1936-39
Bill Whatley (226)   1931-32

Above: A list of the thirty-seven players who played for Northfleet United and then moved on to play in the Football League for Tottenham Hotspur.

Right: Les Bennett (1918–99). Born at Wood Green, this clever inside forward completed only one full season at Northfleet, 1938/39. Les was a member of the team that played Northfleet's very last match before war broke out in September 1939. After the war he became an important member of the Spurs side that won Second and First Division titles in successive seasons, scoring 104 goals in 272 games before enjoying a brief spell at West Ham United prior to retirement.

Les Bennett

Left: Northfleet played their last ever game on 2 September 1939, just a day before war was declared, and it was fitting that the opposition for the Kent League game was the old enemy Dartford. The Fleet won 4–3 to make it three wins out of three for the season – sadly, that was to be it. Gravesend United survived seven years longer and added a third Kent Senior Cup to their honours list in a severely truncated 1944 competition. They played their last game at Ramsgate in April 1946, losing 2–0.

Below: Central Avenue was the fourth ground of Gravesend United following Fairfields, Pelham Road and, for a brief season-long stay following their re-formation in 1932, Milton Barracks. They moved into the Central Avenue ground in 1933 and remained there until their end in 1946. This photograph is taken from where one of the goals once stood, with the opposing goal now swallowed up by housing. The main stand stood on the left and remained there until the late 1970s while the ground was in use by Gravesend Rugby Club. The changing rooms were in the Central Hotel (now the Ascot Arms), out of view on the right.

Sid Tickridge

Above left: Sid Tickridge (1923–97). Stepney-born Sid came to Stonebridge Road as a sixteen-year-old in 1939 and played at full-back in the club's last ever match before war was declared. He was the final Spurs player to come off the Northfleet conveyor belt. After the war he played nearly 100 times for Spurs before moving on to Chelsea and later Brentford.

Above right: Joe Lingham (1870–1943). Very much Mr Northfleet United, Joe was a founder member of the club as a twenty-year-old player. His building company at 1 The Hill, Northfleet, made him a rich man and also benefited the club as it was they who erected the main stand, opened in 1920. Joe became chairman of the club in 1906, a role he kept for most of his life before becoming president. He was also a prominent member of the Kent County Football Association and Northfleet – and football – lost a true friend on his death in December 1943.

PRICE TWOPENCE.

Official ⬥ Programme.

KENT COUNTY FOOTBALL ASSOCIATION.

KENT SENIOR CUP—FINAL TIE.

EASTER MONDAY, APRIL 10th, 1944.

Kick off 3.15 p.m.

GRAVESEND.

Goal.
M. BENNETT.
1

Backs.
R. WADE.   E. COLLINS.
2   3

Half-Backs.
J. DANIELS.   S. VENESS.   W. LUMBY.
4   5   6

Forwards.
L. FELL.   M. DANIELS.   R. EWERS.   R. COLLINS.   W. JESSOP.
7   8   9   10   11

12   13   14   15   16
C. LEYFIELD. L/Bdr. A. R. LOWES. Gnr. F. J. KURZ. Gnr. A. SOMERFIELD. Gnr. A. DRIVER.
Forward.

17   18   19
Sergt. L. SALMON.   Gnr. G. MATTHEWSON.   Bdr. J. BRAIN.
Half-Backs.

20   21
Bdr. H. FERRIER.   Bdr. D. WINTER.
Backs.

22
Sergt. W. A. HUGHES.
Goal.

R.A. DEPOT, WOOLWICH (Holders).
Colours—Red and White, Blue Knickers.
Referee - C. W. CLARK.

Linesman—A. E. FARMER.   *Linesman—W. W. GORHAM.*

Some things are not what they seem, according to the Kent Senior Cup final programme from any given year Gravesend United are the winners of the 1943/44 competition; sadly this is incorrect as Royal Artillery won the game 5–3 to complete a hat-trick of victories. Hopefully by the time the 2011/12 competition is played the KCFA will get their facts right.

Les Fell (1920–2010). Born in Leytonstone, Fell moved to Margate as a youngster when his parents took over a guest house and played for the local side before the outbreak of the Second World War. Working as a draughtsman at Shorts aircraft factory in Rochester, he played as an amateur for the Shrimpers using his speed on the wing to good effect although he ended on the losing side in the 1944 Kent Senior Cup final. Just two years later he would appear in a much more famous final – the FA Cup final for Charlton only to lose again, 4–1 to Derby County after extra time.

Les Fell

3

TOGETHER AT LAST
1946–9

The biggest game thus far in the club's history was the FA Cup first round tie with Torquay United in 1949/50. Entertaining Football League opposition for the first time, the game was well balanced at 1–1 when Eddie Viles (second left) and Charlie Wipfler closed in on a chance only to be foiled by visiting custodian Derek Davis. A crowd of 7,119 saw the Third Division South side go on to clinch a 3–1 victory with two late goals. Thirty years later the Gulls were back again at the same stage of the competition winning 1–0, but good things come to those who wait as in 2008 Fleet beat Torquay in the FA Trophy final at Wembley.

Above: A new beginning as Gravesend & Northfleet line up before their very first match on 31 August 1946 for a Southern League match against the previous season's runners-up Hereford United. The Bulls were to be brushed aside by a 3–0 margin as the new era got off to an exciting start in front of a 6,000 crowd.

ANDREW N. WILSON
CHELSEA

The start of a brand new club on 31 August 1946 saw a disappointing programme issued by Gravesend & Northfleet officials lacking any occasion with just a handful of words welcoming the mayor with the rest of the four pages taken up by advertising. Paper was in short supply at the time but that is hardly an excuse for such a lacklustre effort.

Opposite, bottom: Andy Wilson (1896–1973) was the club's first manager. Born in Newmains, Lanarkshire, he began as a centre forward with Cambuslang Rangers and the sheer weight of goals he scored quickly got him noticed as he moved south to Middlesbrough. His next move was even further south to Chelsea for a record £6,000 fee in 1923. He played 14 times for Scotland, scoring 17 goals – the best ratio of any Scottish player. He moved on to Walsall, where he later became manager. He made light of a serious injury to his arm sustained in the First World War, although the handicap gradually got worse and he was rarely seen without a protective glove. He later played bowls for his adopted country. After a relatively successful first season at Gravesend & Northfleet in 1946/47, disagreements with the board of directors began to emerge and he departed in the close season. His son Jim played for the Fleet during that first season before later moving to Watford.

Gravesend & Northfleet cartoon, 1947/48.

Opposite, top: The reserve side line up for their first ever Kent League game on 7 September 1946 against Royal Marines (Deal). In the background can be seen the Northfleet end at its most rustic – six years before being buried under concrete to build the large Northfleet End stand.

*Opposite, bottom:*Action from that first game as Fleet's Fred Pincott gets the better of Hereford's Thomas in an impressive 3–0 win. Also in the picture is Truxy Wakeman, scorer of one of Fleet's goals who went on to play 202 games and score 75 times in his two spells at the club.

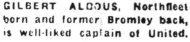

GILBERT ALDOUS, Northfleet born and former Bromley back, is well-liked captain of United.

Above: Gilbert Aldous receives the Kent Senior Cup from R.J. Rule, chairman of the KCFA, after Gravesend & Northfleet finally overcame Gillingham in a second replay. The fact that two of those games took place in the Gills' own Priestfield back yard made the achievement even more creditable. The incredible saga began with a 2–2 draw at Maidstone, watched by 8,250 people; because of demand the replay had to be switched to the largest Kent ground at Priestfield, which was justified by a record-breaking 16,733 crowd to watch a 1–1 draw. Then came the third game and the deadlock was broken in front of 12,633 as the Fleet won 2–0.

Left, above and below: Northfleet-born brothers Stan and Gilbert Aldous were vital cogs in the side that won the Fleet their first trophy: the 1948/49 Kent Senior Cup. Both started their senior careers at Bromley before switching to their home-town team in 1948. Stan played 111 times and scored 3 goals before moving to Leyton Orient where he had further success. He returned as manager (unpaid) in 1967 and had a couple of games as a player – the second oldest to play for Fleet. Gilbert played 76 times and also scored 3 times before suffering a serious injury on Boxing Day 1949 while playing Dartford. He was later given a benefit game and subsequently embarked upon a comeback with Kent League club Ramsgate.

STAN ALDOUS Leyton Orient

Gravesend United's win after dour struggle

Holder's attack faltered on rugged defence

By "TOWNSMAN"

Gillingham, 0; Gravesend and Northfleet, 2.

TIP your hats to one of the strongest and most rugged defences in the Southern League.

It belongs to Gravesend and Northfleet United and, because of that, on Wednesday evening at Priestfield Stadium, they beat the homesters, Gillingham, to win the coveted Kent Senior Cup for the first time in their history.

Gillingham were the better footballing side, but their fast-moving attack got no change out of a defence that never let up and was rarely caught out of position.

It was a game of contrasting styles. Time and again the Gillingham attack, moving with precision and ably prompted by the halves, swept down on the Gravesend goal.

ROCK-LIKE DEFENCE

Each time they were driven back. The challengers' defence was rock steady and solid.

Many defences would have wilted under such continued pressure, but United's stood firm and such good cover did goalie Gould get that he was not often in trouble. Only one shot nearly beat him.

This was when Kingsnorth, in an effort to level the goal he had scored for Gravesend, let fly a beauty. Gould was pleased to push this one round. Cat-like in his movements, uncanny in anticipation, he made the rest look easy.

But Gravesend should have made the game safe in the first half.

After nine minutes a Baldwin-Wipfler move gave Hawkins a chance. His shot hit an upright with Burke beaten.

Later, Gravesend's leader cleverly drew the defence, beat Burke, but then fired over and wide of an open net!

Just before the break—no score—he "blinded" wide. This was real hard luck for a persevering leader.

GILLS BEAT THEMSELVES

At the interval betting was on Gillingham. They always looked better but never seemed able to get there. In short, they beat themselves.

They started off, however, as though they were going to cakewalk matters, but Williams, a shrewd leader who had too much to do, saw his header arrested by Gould's cross-bar. After that Aldous (S.) stuck to him closer than a long-lost brother.

Then, at the other end, Hawkins burst through and was allowed to proceed by the referee. He fired in a shot that entered the net via an upright, but the "goal" was disallowed.

After 55 minutes Gravesend went ahead. It was tragedy for Gillingham. Wipfler crossed a good pass to Wakeman, who had been having some stern duels with the ever-watchful Marks. This time the winger got the better of Marks and returned the ball to Wipfler. Firing into a crowd of players, he saw KINGSNORTH deflect the shot past Burke.

How strange it was that in all of the three games a player had scored against his own side! Gravesend, in the final and first replay, did it on each occasion.

Gillingham, in an effort to draw level, made forward switches, but still that rugged, dogged defence of United's came out on top.

Evergreen Wilson and young Briggs did all they knew. Former Spurs player, Williams, roamed and worked. All to no effect.

WAKEMAN HURT

Then, after Wakeman had been reduced to a hobbling passenger through a knee injury, came curtains for the holders.

Eight minutes to go, Deevey swung across a beautiful centre HAWKINS was waiting and this time he made no mistake, rounding Kingsnorth and beating Burke from close range.

It was all over and Gravesend had won the Cup for the first time.

Let us then give them full marks. Although not as polished as Gillingham, they once again proved themselves a full 90-minute team. Their defence was great, and in it, as the outstanding man, was centre-half Stan Aldous, with the rest very, very close on his heels.

Forward, Gravesend did not have the craft of Gillingham, but Wipfler was always a box of tricks Hawkins should not be dismayed. He, like the rest, never gave up In fact a fine all-round display and a worthy victory.

CUP PRESENTED

Cup and medals were presented by Alderman R. W. Rule, J.P., Chairman, K.C.F.A. Council.

Gravesend and Northfleet Utd.: Gould; Aldous (G.), Chambers; Busby, Aldous (S.), Dimmock; Wakeman, Deevey, Hawkins, Baldwin, Wipfler.

Gillingham: Burke; Dorling, Marks; Boswell, Kingsnorth, Piper; Warsap, Wilson, Williams, Carr; Briggs

Above: The amazing three-match marathon that broke all records for the Kent Senior Cup final was finally decided in Fleet's favour on 31 August 1949. The need for a second replay meant that the game had to be carried into the 1949/50 season.

Above right: Roy Butler was the first Fleet player to score four goals in a game, achieving this in an 8–2 victory over Sittingbourne in the Kent Senior Shield. He had a fine goal ratio of 39 goals in 57 outings in his 1946–8 Fleet career. He later played for Dartford, Tonbridge and Chelmsford and had a successful car sales business in Strood. Roy died in 2001.

Right: Wing half Ted Dimmock was one of the unsung heroes of the team that beat Gillingham to take the Kent Senior Cup in 1949. He made 79 appearances and scored 2 goals in his spell at the club between 1948 and 1951.

A 1949/50 drawing from the excellent but short-lived *Sporting Mirror*. One mystery: why the black and white outfit?

Gravesend Council held a reception at the town hall for the club after their Kent Senior Cup victory in 1949. Captain Gilbert Aldous stands proudly next to the mayor with other members of the team, club officials and the mayoress.

4

THE SMITH AND LOGIE YEARS 1950–9

New player-manager Cliff Edwards looks confident with his 1950/51 side but it was to be a disappointing campaign that saw the team finish eighteenth out of twenty-three sides in the Southern League. Back row, left to right: Ted Harston (trainer), Sam Chambers, Bert Hawkins, Jim Deevey, Tommy James, Percy Skinner, George Baldwin, Tom Peters, Cyril Gould. Front row: Les Gore, Tug Wilson, Cliff Edwards, Eddie Viles, George Fullbrook.

Dick Roche became Fleet's fourth manager in 1951. The forty-five-year-old schoolteacher was a surprise appointment, his main achievement being to produce a string of talented youngsters in youth football. He remained for a year before resigning.

DICK ROCHE.

Bill Whatley

Bill Whatley (1912–74). The Ebbw Vale-born full-back played at Northfleet in 1931/32 helping the club to a Kent League and Cup double. He went on to play more than 200 games for Spurs and was capped for Wales. He returned to Stonebridge Road in 1954 as manager but sadly his youth policy proved disastrous as his string of youngsters proved ill-equipped for the Southern League and he was sacked before the year was out.

1953 Kent Senior Cup winning side
Back Row: Bill McEwan, Ted Harston (Trainer), Charlie Carroll, Jack Flockhart, Tom Baker,
Bill Longdon, Jim Peevey, Unkown, Fred Blowers, Harold Merrison (Director), John Rigg (Director),
Sam Chambers, Bert Hawkins.
Front Row: F. Stevens (Director), Ken Jones, Len Wakeman, Kevin Clarke,
Arthur Norris-Telling (Chairman), Gordon Loukes, Jack Winter, Arthur Rothwell (Driector)

Above and below: The 1952/53 team which won a second Kent Senior Cup with a 2–1 victory over local rivals Dartford, captured in both photographic and cartoon form.

The terrible floods of 31 January 1953 left the Thames Estuary in chaos. There was serious loss of life on the Essex side, notably on Canvey Island, but the Kent side was more fortunate. Amazingly, not a single fixture was lost at Stonebridge Road.

Right and below: The programme from the 1953 Kent Senior Cup final played at Gillingham in which Fleet beat their old rivals Dartford 2–1 in front of 8,876 supporters, Jack Winter and Bill McEwan scoring the goals.

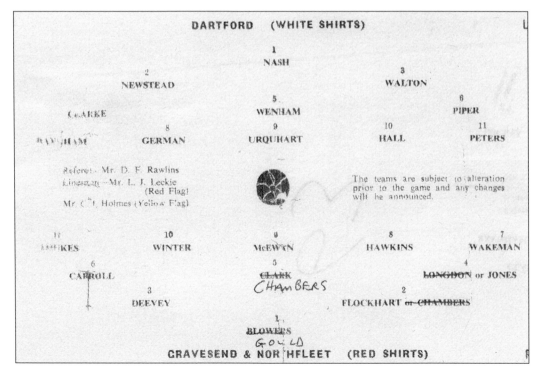

The floodlight trials of winter 1952 are watched by, from left to right, directors Frank Stevens (chairman 1965–7), Arthur Norris-Telling (chairman 1952–9 and 1964–5), John Rigg, A.J. Stevens and Albert Rothwell.

FLOODLIGHT FOOTBALL

MONDAY, 8th NOVEMBER, 1954

Gravesend & Northfleet
v.
Racing Club de Calais

Kick-off 7.30 p.m.

For value ..

Here's the very latest edition of the famous Bush T.V.24, the most 'bought after' 12" set that we handle. It is known as the T.V.24C. As well as those of the B.B.C service, this model is capable of receiving the proposed alternative programmes within whatever proves to be the effective areas of the new transmitters.

54 GNS. (Tax Paid)

Look to your BUSH dealer

Due to reliability and exceptional value, Bush Company are unable to meet the great demand, so order early to save disappointment.

BUSH MAIN DISTRIBUTORS

RAINBOW

PROGRAMME   PRICE THREEPENCE

FLOODLIGHT FOOTBALL

TUESDAY, 8th MARCH, 1955

Gravesend & Northfleet
v.
DUNKERQUOISE

Kick-off 7.30 p.m.

For value ..

Here's the very latest edition of the famous Bush T.V.24, the most 'bought after' 12" set that we handle. It is known as the T.V.24C. As well as those of the B.B.C service, this model is capable of receiving the proposed alternative programmes within whatever proves to be the effective areas of the new transmitters.

54 GNS. (Tax Paid)

Look to your BUSH dealer

Due to reliability and exceptional value, Bush Company are unable to meet the great demand, so order early to save disappointment.

BUSH MAIN DISTRIBUTORS

RAINBOW

PROGRAMME   PRICE THREEPENCE

Right: Jackie Bridge (1932–). Born in Great Wakering, the stylish wing half and dead-eye penalty taker began his career at his local club, Southend, before moving to Gravesend in 1956. A lynchpin in the 1957/58 Southern League title-winning side, he eventually left for Sheppey in 1964 after 380 games and 39 goals, nearly all of them from the penalty spot. He later returned for a brief spell as manager at the start of the 1967/68 season.

Below: The 1955/56 side that finished twelfth in the Southern League. Back row, left to right: Charlie Poulton, Norman Lewis, Sam English, Peter Heathcote, Brian Moule, Sam Chambers. Front row: Lionel Smith, Jimmy Logie, Frank Neary, George Stewart, Jimmy Scarth.

Bob Thomas (1919–90). Born in Stepney, the free-scoring inside forward was top marksman in the 1957/58 title-winning team – just as he had been the previous season when he had picked up a winners' medal with Kettering, along with fellow Fleetman Harry MacDonald. Bob had played for Brentford, Plymouth, Fulham, Crystal Palace and Kettering before joining Fleet. At the end of the 1958/59 season, having scored 82 goals in 104 games, he was allowed to move on to Clacton, whom he inspired to promotion into the Southern League Premier Division.

Lionel Smith (1920–80). Born in Mexborough, Yorkshire, Lionel joined Arsenal from Denaby United in 1939, playing 162 games for the Gunners and winning both a Football League Championship and an FA Cup as well as earning several England international caps at full-back in a career considerably reduced by war. He moved on to Watford and then joined Fleet as player-manager in January 1955. A persistent knee injury restricted him to just 12 appearances before retirement allowed him to concentrate on his managerial role. His strong connections in the game enabled him to sign many quality players and Fleet swept to the Southern League title in 1957/58. Sadly, at the end of the 1959/60 season he decided against renewing his contract and moved into the licensing trade, never to manage a football team again.

Arguably the best side to ever put on the Fleet's red shirt and certainly the most entertaining, the 1957/58 championship side proved once again that stability rather than constant changes makes for a successful side. In a 42-match league programme only nineteen players were used, and seven of those made only single-figure appearances, with eleven of the team making 30 appearances or more. All the regulars are included in this photo except that the unlucky Sam Chambers made only five appearances before injury kept him out and he was replaced by Sam English. Back row, left to right: Lionel Smith (manager), Charlie Carson, Arthur Shaw (captain), Jackie Bridge, Peter Heathcote, Sam Chambers, Joe Thompson, Harry MacDonald, Dave Thomas (trainer). Front row: Jimmy Scarth, Jimmy Logie, Eric Day, Bob Thomas, Jimmy Robertson.

The new signings for 1957/58 line up at the pre-season photo call. It would be a highly contrasting season for the players, the four on the left, Derek Styles, Mick Martin, Tommy Tilston and Eddie Lyons managed just four appearances between them (although local lad Styles would eventually play more than 50 games over the next few seasons), while Bob Thomas and Eric Day scored over 80 goals between them during the season and Harry MacDonald would provide many years of outstanding service at left-back and would be the only link between this championship-winning side and the FA Cup giant-killing side of 1962/63.

Harry MacDonald (1926–2004). Born in Salford, this stylish left-back moved south to Crystal Palace in 1950 from Ashton United before moving on to Kettering in 1955. Having won a Southern League title with the Poppies in 1956/57, he then did likewise with the Fleet and was the only player who appeared in both that success and the giant-killing cup side of 1962/63. Harry retired at the end of 1963/64 and had a very successful benefit game as befitted a highly popular and loyal player who clocked up 308 appearances but never scored a goal.

Jimmy Logie

Jimmy Logie (1919–84). The wee Scot – just 5ft 4in – was born in Edinburgh and began with Lochore Welfare before moving to Arsenal just three months before war broke out in 1939. He eventually made 296 appearances and scored 68 goals for the Gunners, winning both League and FA Cup medals and a single Scotland cap. His signing for Gravesend in January 1955 was a major coup as a string of clubs had chased his signature and Fleet were rock bottom of the Southern League at the time. With Logie at thirty-five it looked likely to be a short-term deal, but he played for five seasons and helped the club go from bottom to top before retiring in December 1959 to take over the Greyhound, Stoke Newington. He had played 217 games and scored 47 goals and remains probably the best player to don a Fleet shirt.

A new season always brings hope and the 1958/59 season began with Fleet proudly holding the Southern League championship trophy (on display above the directors' box). They are shown on the attack against visitors Bedford who had finished runners-up to Fleet but got the better in this game, winning 5–2 – hardly the dream start expected. Note the lack of shirt sleeves from the August crowd and the bench looks extremely underpopulated with just trainer Dave Thomas itching to use his magic sponge and bucket of water. Substitutes were still eight years away so no chance of much company from them and manager Lionel Smith is sitting in the directors' box.

November 1958 saw Fleet chasing Bedford for the title and entertaining and beating Yeovil Town 4–3 with Bob Thomas hurdling over David Jones in the Glovers' goal. The covering of the Stonebridge Road side is almost complete with the late lamented Black Eagle public house in clear view. In 2012 the Fleet Trust announced an appeal to re-roof the stand and much of the profit from this book will be going to the cause.

The programme from the infamous Boxing Day game of 1959 which saw a senior game abandoned through fighting for the first time ever. Referee Ron Sturgeon had been a linesman the previous day when an ill-tempered game had ended in a 4–2 victory for the Darts at Stonebridge Road. As a police traffic cop he was clearly used to dishing out the discipline and after 80 minutes with the Darts leading 2–0 he abandoned the game for alleged fighting although most bystanders and the players were amazed at the decision. On Friday 15 January 1960 both clubs were summoned to Lancaster Gate to face an FA disciplinary committee who concluded that the conduct of the players were such to bring the game into disrepute and the referee was justified in abandoning the game by the power invested in him. They were also unhappy that the management of the clubs had done nothing after the first game to instruct their players as to their conduct. Despite what appears to be a damning decision against both parties, there were no fines other than the costs of the tribunal (awarded against the clubs). There was a warning as to the future conduct of both clubs and that the game should be replayed.

The next meeting of the two clubs came in early March with a Kent Senior Cup tie. Fleet centre-half Sam English can be seen beating Tommy Huckstepp to the ball and clearing his lines. Jackie Bridge takes cover and goalkeeper Norman Coe and full-back Barry Judges look on. The Darts won 3–1 in front of a 3,181 crowd.

The 1959/60 side line up before the FA Cup fourth qualifying round tie with Ashford. Disappointment was waiting as, for the third year running, they fell at the final hurdle before the competition proper, losing 2–1. Back row, left to right: Jimmy Robertson, Harry MacDonald, Sam English, Jackie Bridge, Norman Coe, Charlie Carson, Jimmy Fletcher, Dave Thomas (trainer). Front row: Jimmy Scarth, Jimmy Logie, Alan Brown, Kevin Baron, Johnny Simmonds.

Alan Brown (1935–). Born in Rainworth, Nottinghamshire, Alan was the only Gravesend & Northfleet player to play Test cricket although Harry Howell (see page 15) did so for Northfleet United. Alan is seen here in 1959.

5

GIANT-KILLING, RELEGATION AND MONEY TROUBLES 1960–9

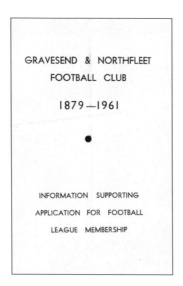

GRAVESEND & NORTHFLEET
FOOTBALL CLUB

1879 — 1961

INFORMATION SUPPORTING

APPLICATION FOR FOOTBALL

LEAGUE MEMBERSHIP

In both 1960/61 and 1961/62, the club somewhat optimistically applied for election to the Football League. To do so meant sweet-talking all 92 Football League clubs and providing them with a glossy brochure extolling the virtues of the club and telling a few porkies along the way, such as being founded in 1879 rather than 1946, having beaten Spurs 8–0 in a Southern League game and telling them of a '16,000 crowd capacity with much more room for expansion and a car park holding 450 cars'. Projects in hand were 'a new building costing £10,000 incorporating offices, board room, social hall and gymnasium'. This waffle would have made any politician happy but sadly at both AGMs, Fleet failed to get a vote.

Ron Humpston (1923–) was a Derby-born goalkeeper who played for Portsmouth and Huddersfield before moving abroad to coach. He was appointed manager of Gravesend in 1960 with the difficult task of following the popular and successful Lionel Smith. Ron's bold policy was to give youth its chance, and while this was highly creditable and initially successful, the team gradually faded and only just avoided relegation on goal average. Matters failed to improve during the early months of the 1961/62 season and he was sacked in November 1961.

An improvised assault course was erected in the club car park by new manager Ron Humpston for pre-season training in 1960 to help fitness. Leading the way are reserve team players Brian Homersham, Ivan Clarke and John Tank.

Ernie Walley

Above left: On 25 March 1961, for the first and only time, the Football League came to Stonebridge Road when Gillingham met Wrexham in a Fourth Division game won by the Welsh side 3–0. The reason the game was played at Northfleet was the closing of Priestfield by the FA following a pitch invasion by spectators in which the referee was knocked to the ground after the Gills had lost to Oldham Athletic. Thirty-nine years later the Gills were able to return the favour when the FA Cup first round game between Gravesend and Notts County was transferred to Priestfield after constant postponements owing to waterlogging.

Above right: Ernie Walley (1933–) was born in Caernarfon and signed for Tottenham in 1951 but managed only six appearances in five years. The stylish wing half moved to Middlesbrough and then on to Guildford City, from whom he joined the Fleet in November 1961. Ernie featured strongly in the FA Cup giant-killing side of 1962/63 and made 77 appearances for the club, scoring 6 goals, before moving to Stevenage at the end of the 1962/63 season.

Boxing Day 1962 was not one to remember. It was bad enough that the Southern League had sent them to Worcester but much worse came when the first snowfalls of what was to be a bitter winter turned the game into a farce. Even worse, relegation looked even more likely after this 3–1 defeat. In this picture Tony Cottrill's shot is blocked by Tony Newcombe while Johny Sanchez looks on. It was well past midnight when the team arrived home in Kent.

55

GRAVESEND & NORTHFLEET F.C.
LIMITED

Associate Members Football Association, Kent County F.A.,
Members Southern League and Metropolitan League

Directors:
H. MERRISON, *Chairman;* A. C. NORRIS-TELLING, *Vice-Chairman;* A. E. ROTHWELL,
F. STEVENS, H. J. TOWN, S. G. GRAY
Secretary: G. E. FOOKS.   *Hon. Treasurer:* A. E. ROTHWELL
Manager: W. H. C. LANE
Ground: STONEBRIDGE ROAD, NORTHFLEET. Tel.—Gravesend 3796
Colours: RED SHIRTS, WHITE COLLARS, WHITE SHORTS

No. 4   OFFICIAL PROGRAMME   № 926

F.A. CUP—1st Round Qualifying
SATURDAY, SEPTEMBER 8, 1962

Gravesend & Northfleet
v.
Chatham

Kick-off 3 p.m.

STAN'S BACK

"ONLY MANAGING"

1 MAY AVENUE,
NORTHFLEET,
GRAVESEND, KENT.

ALDOUS BROS.

PORTABLE BUILDINGS   FENCING AND TIMBER

GRAVESEND & NORTHFLEET F.C.
LIMITED

Associate Members Football Association, Kent County F.A.,
Members Southern League and Metropolitan League

Directors:
H. MERRISON, *Chairman;* A. C. NORRIS-TELLING, *Vice-Chairman;* A. E. ROTHWELL,
F. STEVENS, H. J. TOWN, S. G. GRAY
Secretary: G. E. FOOKS.   *Hon. Treasurer:* A. E. ROTHWELL
Manager: W. H. C. LANE
Ground: STONEBRIDGE ROAD, NORTHFLEET. Tel.—Gravesend 3796
Colours: RED SHIRTS, WHITE COLLARS, WHITE SHORTS

No. 21   OFFICIAL PROGRAMME

F.A. CUP—4th Round Proper

Gravesend & Northfleet
v.
Sunderland

Kick-off 7.30 p.m.

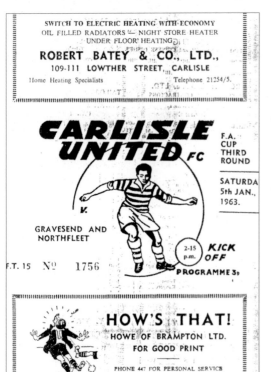

CARLISLE UNITED FC
v.
GRAVESEND AND
NORTHFLEET

F.A. CUP THIRD ROUND

SATURDAY
5th JAN.,
1963.

2-15 p.m.   KICK OFF

F.T. 15   № 1756   PROGRAMME 3d.

SEASON 1962-63   OFFICIAL PROGRAMME

4D

SUNDERLAND
ASS'N FOOTBALL CLUB LTD · ROKER PARK

No. 31

F.A. CUP WINNERS — 1937
DIV. 1 LEAGUE CHAMPIONS
1891-92   1892-93   1894-95
1901-02   1912-13   1935-36

F.A. CUP—4th ROUND
REPLAY

Sunderland
v.
Gravesend & Northfleet

Kick-off 7-15 p.m.

Harry Easton (1938–). Born in Shoreham, the former Crystal Palace player was a mainstay of the 1962/63 FA Cup giant-killing side with his busy forward play and was one of the few survivors the following season when the club again did well, losing unluckily 1–0 at Brentford in the second round. Easton played 83 times scoring 19 goals between 1962 and 1964.

Tension around the Fleet goalmouth as Wycombe apply pressure in the FA Cup second round of 1962/63. Harry MacDonald covers the line as Alan Humphreys dives. Fleet won the match 3–1 to reach the third round for the first time ever.

Opposite, above left: The record-breaking FA Cup run began on 8 September 1962 with a less-than-convincing 2–1 win over Chatham Town and ended five months and ten days later at Sunderland on 18 February 1963. This was the longest time any club had been involved in the competition in its near-100-year history and, although Blyth Spartans exactly equalled the achievement with their great run of 1977/78, the record has never been beaten in the 125 years of the FA Cup.

Opposite, above right and bottom: Three more programmes from that great cup run. The Carlisle match due to take place on 5 January was eventually staged, after five postponements, on 29 January and it can be noted that neither of the Gravesend v Sunderland matches had a scheduled date on the programme because cancellations were expected owing to the constant weather problems. As it turned out, this happened with the first game but not the replay.

Magic under the Stonebridge Road floodlights as a record 12,032 cram into the ground. 14,000 tickets were printed for the game but such were the terrible conditions in the bleakest winter on record that Sunderland supporters were unable to travel. The snow and slush cleared from the pitch can be seen in front of the fence on the packed Sonebridge Road side. The photo shows Fleet's outstanding centre-half Tony Newcombe challenging Sunderland's Scottish international George Herd.

The end of a great night as Harry Easton hugs Tony Sitford as the crowd gets ready to invade the pitch.

Another Micky Durling drawing, this time of the Gravesend v Sunderland game which attracted a ground record 12,032 to Stonebridge Road on 12 February 1963 to see a 1–1 draw in the fourth round.

Bobby Cameron (1932–). This Greenock-born inside forward was another cup hero of 1962/63. His stylish play at Port Glasgow tempted Queens Park Rangers to bring him south and he made 256 appearances between 1950 and 1958 before moving on to Leeds United. Bobby joined the Fleet in 1962 as one of several full-time players. A troublesome knee injury restricted him to 41 appearances and 7 goals before he moved back into the Football League briefly with Southend in October 1963. He later emigrated to Australia, where he still lives.

Chester-born Alan Humphreys (1939–) was a goalkeeper who seemed destined for the top when playing 32 times for Shrewsbury as a teenager before moving on to Leeds and earning England Under-23 caps. But after two years at Leeds, in which injuries restricted him to just 40 appearances, he moved south to join Gravesend as a full-timer. Again injury reduced his appearances and, after playing in all the FA Cup games of 1962, the games at Carlisle and Sunderland saw his deputy Peter Reader step into the breach. In all, he played 44 times for the club before getting back into the Football League and playing more than 100 times for Mansfield and Chesterfield, showing what a good goalkeeper he was.

Brian Skingley (1937–99). Born in Romford, Brian played originally at full-back, signing for Bristol Rovers and then moving on to Crystal Palace without breaking through to claim a regular spot at either club. His boisterous style led him to also playing at centre forward – a position he filled perfectly at Stonebridge Road after signing in November 1962. He made himself an instant hit with the fans by scoring a hat-trick in only his second match and then scoring twice against Wycombe to put Fleet through to the third round of the FA Cup. He then laid on the winner for Tony Sitford at Carlisle and scored the goal that saw Stonebridge Road erupt against Sunderland, a game in which he sustained an injury that saw him miss the replay at a time when he was at the peak of his career. He left at the end of the season but returned briefly in 1968/69. In all, he made 45 appearances and scored 12 goals for the club.

Bob McNicol (1933–80). Dumbarton-born Bob was one of the Fleet's giant-killing heroes of the 1962/63 season. He was a rugged full-back who had played more than 200 Football League games for Accrington Stanley and Brighton, from whom he joined Fleet as one of a new breed of full-time players in 1962. In an eventful cup run he scored the winner to put Exeter out in the first round and also scored at Sunderland before being sent off. He left for Carlisle in October 1963 after playing 62 games and scoring 4 goals for the club. He was sadly killed in a plane crash in Tenerife in 1980.

The great marathon cup run finally came off the rails at an icy Roker Park against Sunderland in a fourth-round replay on 18 February 1963. Centre half Tony Newcombe, the club's outstanding defender of the '60s, helps foil another Sunderland attack.

Everybody except goalkeeper Peter Reader is having trouble staying on his feet. The Fleet players are Harry MacDonald (far left) and Tony Newcombe (far right).

Right: Brothers Brian (left) and John Roche line up before the 1964/65 season. They had contrasting fortunes with Brian playing only four times on the left wing without scoring, while inside forward John top-scored in his single season with the club, netting 10 goals in 42 games. He had earlier played for Millwall, Crystal Palace and Margate. He later made further history when his son, also John, played for Fleet 16 times during the 1986/87 season. They were the first of three father and son duos to play for the club; Pip and Danny Jeffrey and Bob and Danny Glozier later also achieved this feat.

Below: Gravesend were desperately unlucky to lose 1–0 at Brentford in the second round of the FA Cup on 7 December 1963. Here Mike Wilkins tries his luck at goal watched by Harry Easton, a survivor of the great cup run of the previous season. Mel Scott takes evasive action for the Bees.

Jim Towers (1933–2010). Born in Shepherds Bush, 'Big Jim' scored nearly 200 Football League goals for Brentford, Queens Park Rangers, Millwall, Gillingham and Aldershot and scored five in a game against Gravesend & Northfleet while playing for Romford, from whom Fleet signed him in 1965. Although past his best, his thunderous shooting over the next two seasons made him a great crowd favourite as he scored 48 goals in 87 matches in a struggling team. Big Jim retired early in the 1967/68 season as injuries took their toll.

George Waites (1938–2000) was a Stepney-born inside forward who had played for Leyton Orient, Norwich and Brighton before joining Fleet in 1965. He scored 21 goals in 109 games in a three-year stay in which, along with Jim Towers, he was a mainstay of the forward line.

Barry Fry (1945–). Born in Bedford, this schoolboy international appeared to have a great career ahead of him and joined Manchester United, but was never able to establish himself. After short, equally unsuccessful spells at Bolton and Luton he found himself at Stonebridge Road in 1966. He quickly found form and when Walter Rickett left to become assistant manager at Leyton Orient he quickly returned to bring Fry with him. Fry had played just 20 matches and scored 2 goals for the Fleet from midfield. He later became much better known as a manager at Barnet, Maidstone, Southend, Birmingham and Peterborough.

Barry Fry scores a goal against Wisbech in a 2–2 draw in October 1966 but soon he would be following manager Walter Rickett to Leyton Orient.

Walter Rickett (1917–91). Born in Sheffield, Rickett was a winger who played for Sheffield Wednesday and Blackpool and whose career highlight was playing on the opposite wing to Stanley Matthews in the 1948 FA Cup final when Blackpool lost to Manchester United 4–2. He later played for Sheffield United, Halifax and Rotherham before moving south and managing Ramsgate and Sittingbourne, taking over at Stonebridge Road in 1963. He is pictured leaving Stonebridge Road for the last time in November 1966 after handing in his resignation to take up the assistant manager role at Leyton Orient. Note the canopy which made the ground look grander but was taken down in 1999 because it had become unsafe.

John Dick (1930–2000). This Glasgow-born inside forward had an excellent career with West Ham, where he played 326 games and scored 153 goals between 1953 and 1962, and then played 72 games and scored 44 times for Brentford. Sadly, on signing for Fleet his career was dogged by injury. He took over from the departing manager Walter Rickett in October 1966 with a job description of coach rather than manager but, with black financial clouds again gathering, his task was hopeless and he departed at the end of the season having played just 10 games and scored 3 goals.

Johnny Dick

Former Ashford and Wimbledon goalkeeper Eddie McAlpine signed for Fleet in 1967 and became the third manager of the season at a time when the club were at their lowest ebb. He did improve matters slightly in his player-manager role but broke his leg playing against Corby in 1968 and was sacked a month later.

Alan Jones was a solid defender who made 109 appearances between 1965 an 1968 before breaking his leg against his former club Wisbech in November 1967. At the time the club was rock bottom of the Southern League and could ill afford to lose such an influential player. His comeback attempts failed and he retired in 1968.

Alan Crudace was a great servant of the club through some pretty rough times. The South Shields-born defender signed from Hastings in 1965 and remained until 1973 amassing 394 games and scoring 8 goals before returning to his home-town club.

Alf Ackerman (1929–88). South African-born Alf had an impressive goal tally in his playing career as a centre forward with Clyde, Norwich, Hull, Derby, Carlisle and Millwall. He began his managerial career with Dartford and was surprisingly sacked after four relatively successful seasons. After a break he was persuaded back into the game by his fellow newsagent, Fleet chairman Vic Troke, and as manager helped put Fleet back on the road to success after the grim days of the mid- and late 1960s, earning promotion back to the Southern League Premier Division. He eventually left in March 1974 having groomed his assistant Tony Sitford to take over. Alf returned to South Africa and died there in 1988.

Stan Aldous

Stan Aldous (1923–95) was Northfleet-born and one of the most successful players to come from the area. A solid, no-nonsense centre half, he began his career at Bromley with brother Gilbert before moving back to his home-town club at the tail end of the 1947/48 season. His fine displays were a major factor in the club winning their first honour in 1948/49 with the Kent Senior Cup success over Gillingham. He moved on to Leyton Orient in 1950 and played 302 games for them, including skippering the side to the Third Division (South) title and promotion. After a spell at Headington he went into business owning a factory in Northfleet and became Fleet manager (unpaid) in 1967/68. The club were in desperate financial trouble and were rock bottom of the Southern League – and even Stan couldn't turn this situation around. He even had to play himself briefly, bringing his overall tally of games for the club to 111, with 3 goals.

The town's first open air beat festival
But what happened to all those 'switched-on' teenagers?

A 'FLIP-FLOP' RAVE NIGHT

"YOU'RE not a big audience but you're a groovy one," said showman Freddie Mack as the rain came trickling down over Northfleet football ground on Saturday night.

Gravesend's first open air beat festival went "flip-flop" in a mixture of rain and apathy. Where did the beat fans go? That was the big mystery. They did not go to Northfleet.

When the gates opened at mid-day, only a trickle of people came in. As the concert throbbed on through its 12 hours, the numbers did increase until about 300 chanced the rain to watch "Deep Purple" and finally dance the night out to Freddie Mack.

Toadstool

The 30-foot long double stage was set and reset with microphones, amplifiers and yards of cable. Tea and "Coke" flowed from the refreshment huts, potato puffs were fried on the stands and psychedelic light man "Fairy" on a toadstool of scaffold was invited to project nude ladies on the stage back-screen.

But what was the use when the people it was all for just stayed away?

"I don't know what went wrong," said Colin Howard, one of the three organisers. "Nobody came. There seemed to be so much interest but why nobody turned up I just do not know."

The concert-goers who did take a cold seat on the grass or stand under a field of umbrellas (apart from those hidden away in dark corners for obvious reasons) were there to listen and there was not even a hint of trouble except for a few swear words thrown at the stage.

Freddie Mack soon vetoed that, especially when word went round that he is sparring with Henry Cooper for his next big bout.

Grumbles did come from Wallis Park about the noise and across the valley in Swanscombe there was talk of a complaint of a noisy dance at Manor Road that turned out to be the concert echoing through the cement dust.

Property

In terms of £—s—d the result was the organisers being out of pocket, maybe even up to £500; Gravesend and Northfleet Football Club with a very useful donation plus no serious damage to the pitch or property and at least 300 young people remembering a good night out for ten bob.

OPEN AIR
BEAT FESTIVAL
12-HOUR NON-STOP SPECTACULAR
on SATURDAY, 30th AUGUST
12 MIDDAY — 12 MIDNIGHT
To be held at
GRAVESEND & NORTHFLEET FOOTBALL GROUND
TOP GROUPS INCLUDE
FREDDIE MAC EXTRAVAGANZA
DEEP PURPLE
THE WAY   THE MAGNA
THE FRINGE   SHADRAK VIRGIN
RAMSIES PROPHECY
PLUS DISCOTHEQUES
HOT SNACKS AVAILABLE
ADMISSION ONLY 10/-
ADVANCE TICKETS 9/-
Available at SOUND CENTRE, 9 QUEEN STREET
For Party Bookings Tel. Gravesend 2891

Stonebridge Road has been used for some diverse subjects, from baseball in the First World War to music concerts with renowned rockers Deep Purple appearing in 1969 when open-air concerts were all the rage – sadly it proved a flop.

6

ON THE UP
1970–9

A great start to the new decade as promotion back to the Southern League Premier Division is achieved by the 1970/71 side, who finished third.

Allan Jones did the circuit of Kent clubs as an aggressive centre forward. His single season at Stonebridge Road in 1970/71 proved highly effective, spearheading a successful promotion bid and top-scoring with 19 goals from 43 matches. This included a hat-trick in a 4–1 FA Cup victory over Chatham where he is pictured on the right of the three players in the foreground wearing Fleet's rather unfamiliar garb of all red, which was used during that season.

Colin Blaber was an influential midfielder signed from Crawley who played 112 times between 1972 and 1975. Sadly, he suffered a broken leg on the successful run in to the Southern League South title in 1974/75, which ended his Fleet career.

'My best moment of 17 years in football', was how Manager Tony Sitford described the presentation to him of a watch by the 'Fleet players before the final game of the season. From left to right: Back row, Pip Jeffrey, Mickey Angel, Johnny Thurgood, Dave Bostock, Phil Debnam, Colin Norman, John Cowen, Kenny Burrett. Front row, Brian Woolfe, Les Hall, Ken Pearce, Tony Weston, 'The Boss' Tony Sitford, Colin Blaber, Ray Hutchins.

Above left: Edmonton-born Lee Smelt (1958–) began his career at Colchester and moved on to Margate, from whom Tony Sitford snapped him up in September 1976. He went on to become perhaps Gravesend's greatest goalkeeper. Only eighteen when he began his Fleet career, he made 208 appearances for the club, featuring in the Southern League Cup-winning side and the team that made the Alliance Premier League. Lee moved to Nottingham Forest for £15,000 and then on to Cardiff, Halifax and Peterborough before returning to Kent football with Welling and Margate, whom he later managed.

Above right: Steve Brown makes the vital breakthrough in extra time to give Gravesend the lead against Weymouth in the 1977/78 Southern League Cup final. The first leg in Dorset had ended goalless and another ninety minutes at Stonebridge Road had done likewise. When Brian Woolfe headed a second the cup was Fleet's for the first time.

The outstanding side of 1977/78. Back row, left to right: Brian Hawkes, John Hawker, David Hockley, Jack Bennett, Fred Wilmshurst, Trevor Bonneywell (all directors). Middle row: Danny Keenan (trainer), Andy Woon, Dave Bostock, Ken Burrett, Lee Smelt, Bob Dudman, Graham Byford, Colin Priestley. Front row: Alan Fagan, Steve Brown, Geoff Idle, Roger Easterby (chairman), George Jacks, Tony Sitford (manager), Brian Woolfe, Norman Fusco, Bob Finch.

Ken Burrett (1950–). Born in Camberwell, Burrett signed from Faversham in 1971 and finally retired in 1984 after 504 games and 26 goals as a great defensive stalwart. Geoff Idle (1950–) was born in Fulham signed from Bexley United in 1976. He was a stylish-full back and made 299 appearances with 5 goals earning Southern League Cup and Kent Senior Cup winners medals. Kenny also won a Southern League South winners' medal.

George Jacks (1946–). Born in Whitechapel, Jacks was a competitive midfielder who joined Fleet in 1976 following long spells with Millwall and Gillingham. He was instrumental in the success of the late 1970s and early 1980s before moving on to Barking in 1981 – was it coincidence that Fleet's decline began soon after? He played 237 games and scored 12 goals.

Bob Glozier raises the cup in front of delighted Fleet fans.

Phil Stonebridge was a vital signing from Maidstone to help ensure Gravesend qualified for the newly formed Alliance Premier League. He top-scored in each of his three seasons with the club (1978–81), in all scoring 46 goals in 151 appearances before moving on to Tonbridge.

Alan Hart (1956–). This Woolwich-born midfielder began as an apprentice at Charlton and moved on to Millwall, making a handful of Football League appearances for both clubs before joining Dulwich Hamlet. He joined the Fleet in time for the club's first season in the Alliance League in 1979 and soon settled down, making a midfield berth his own. He played through to the end of 1984/85, by which time he had racked up 214 appearances and 25 goals.

7

DOWN, DOWN AND UP
1980–9

After a twenty-eight-year, wait the Kent Senior Cup is won in 1981
with a 2–0 victory over Ashford Town at Maidstone with goals from
Charlie Pooley and Gary Aldous. Captain Geoff Idle is chaired around
the ground by Jeff Bryant and Charlie Pooley.

FINAL

Chatham Reliance
Building Society
ASSETS EXCEED £50 MILLION
Member of the Building Societies Association

Ashford Town Colours: All Green	**Gravesend & Northfleet** Colours: Red & White
1 PETER CARMEN	1 COLIN LEWINGTON
2 CLIVE HICKSON	2 GEOFF IDLE
3 PETER McROBERT	3 GEORGE JACKS
4 TIM HOGBEN	4 KEN BURRETT
5 JOHN BARROW	5 JEFF BRYANT
6 GRAHAM JORDAN	6 ALAN HART
7 ADRIAN CARTER	7 BOB DUDMAN
8 KEVIN RAYNOR	8 ~~GARY WILLIAMS~~ DYER
9 JOHN YOUNG	9 CHARLIE POOLEY
10 PETER AMBLER	10 PHIL STONEBRIDGE
11 MICKY JOWETT	11 ~~TREVOR SMITH~~ ALDOUS
Sub: DES PARTINGTON	Sub: ~~GARRY ALDOUS~~ WILLIAMS

Referee: R. J. Clements (Tonbridge)

Linesmen: J. B. Roffey (Ashford) Red flag

M. T. Denman (Bexleyheath) Yellow flag

PRIOR to the game both teams and the officials will be presented to Mr D. J. C. Gilchrist, Director of the Chatham Reliance Building Society and to Mr J. Blackburn, Chairman of the Kent County Football Association. The KCFA/Chatham Reliance Building Society Senior Cup will be presented by Mr Gilchrist.

Left: Liverpool-born former Everton, Bradford City, Swindon, Carlisle and Birmingham central defender Stan Harland (1940–2001). After Southern League experience as player-manager of Yeovil, he was brought to Gravesend in a last throw of the dice to try to avoid relegation from the Alliance League in February 1982, but the ploy failed and he left early in 1982/83 along with chairman Roger Easterby, who had brought him to the club.

Below: The 1983/84 side that exceeded expectations by finishing fourth in the Southern League Premier Division – the club's highest position. Back row, left to right: Fred Wilmshurst (director), Andy Wallace, Trevor Bonneywell (director), John Palfreman (secretary), David Hockley (vice chairman), Gary Aldous, Daryl Lucas (assistant secretary), Tom Jenner (director). Middle row: Gary Julians, Steve Hermitage, Trevor Burke, Ken Burrett, Roger Kent, Kelvin Bright, Geoff Eyers, Alan Risk, Geoff Idle, Mick Ward (physio). Front row: Paul Everest, Steve Brignall, Tony Burns (manager), Ray Tumbridge, Lionel Ball (chairman), Kevin Wallis, Alan Hart.

Right: Tony Burns (1944–), born in Edenbridge, was manager of Gravesend from 1982 to 1985 after a fine career as a goalkeeper with his local club Tonbridge and then Arsenal, Brighton, Charlton, Crystal Palace, Brentford and Plymouth, with a four-year spell in South Africa sandwiched in between. His managerial career also began at Tonbridge and after he left Fleet without having collected any trophies he had a further spell with them.

● *Gravesend and Northfleet Football Club illustrated by Mickey Durling.*

From the late 1940s the caricatures of Mickey Durling became legendary in the area and extended onto the national scene. This one of Fleet's 1986/87 team was the last he did for the club who finished sixth in Southern League South. Mickey, a Gravesend resident, died in 1991.

Alan Risk (1964–). Only seventeen when he broke into Fleet's Alliance team as a central defender, Alan played for the club for four seasons, making 128 appearances and scoring a single goal. Always in demand because of his calm, assured displays, he moved to Dagenham in 1985 but injuries blighted his later years.

As the son of Len Julians, a fine marksman for Arsenal and Millwall, Gary Julians always had a lot to live up to and he certainly proved prolific, even though it was at a lower level. In two spells with Gravesend & Northfleet (1983–4 and 1988–90) he scored 36 goals in 123 games.

Paul Burnham holds up the Player of the Year trophy in 1984. Signed from Tonbridge, his goalkeeping in two spells with Fleet (1982–5 and 1990–2) was always of a high standard in 168 games.

Colin Dalton played 269 games as a central defender for Fleet from 1983 to 1991 and is seen challenging Welling's prolific marksman Gary Abbott, who himself played a handful of games for Gravesend towards the end of a long career.

Above left: Liverpool-born Alan Whittle (1950–) won a Football League Championship medal with Everton while still in his teens and later played for Crystal Palace and Leyton Orient before finishing his career with a season at Gravesend in 1984/85, making 14 appearances and scoring once.

Above right: Terry Naylor (1948–). Born in Islington, this full-back or central defender played more than 300 times for Tottenham and Charlton between 1969 and 1983 before finishing his senior career at Gravesend in 1984/85 making 47 appearances and scoring once.

8

MORE UPS AND DOWNS
1990–9

Prolific marksman Steve Portway always had respect from defenders. Here he is closely
watched by Fisher defenders shortly before signing for Gloucester City in a £17,500 move in
November 1994.

Simon Ullathorne was a much-travelled winger who joined Gravesend from Croydon in November 1991 but was a native of Cumbria, having previously played for Workington and Cleator Moor Celtic. Simon played a major role in the promotion side of 1993/94. He played 123 games and scored 17 goals for the club before moving to Hastings in 1994.

Matt Gubbins was another important member of that promotion side with some impressive displays in central defence. Signed from Ashford in November 1992, he played 151 games, scoring twice, and played a key role in the FA Cup run of 1995/96.

Steve Portway often classed this as his most memorable goal – a diving header to put Fleet ahead at Leyton Orient in the first round of the 1993/4 FA Cup. Although the Os came back to win 2–1, Steve had backed himself to score the first goal and made a considerable wedge as a result.

Above: Champions! Fleet players pose in front of delighted supporters after being presented with the Southern League South Division shield in 1994.

Left: Tom Warrilow was the inspirational captain of the 1993/94 promotion side. He had three different spells with the club between 1982 and 1996.

Two all-time Fleet heroes: record goalscorer Steve Portway and record appearance maker Ken Burrett, as Ken presents Steve with the Player of the Year trophy.

Above: The club's best attacking combination for many years was that of Steve Portway and behind him Mickey Cotter. Together they were the scourge of the opposition in the early 1990s.

Right: Gary Aldous had six different spells as a player with the club between 1980 and 1991 and also had a four-year spell as manager from 1991 to 1995. In 118 appearances for the club he scored 27 goals.

Few would have guessed when Godalming were crushed by a record 7–0 scoreline that the road would finally end at Villa Park four months later. Here Mark Munday fires in one of the goals.

Peter Mortley cracks home a spectacular second goal to give Fleet a shock 2–0 victory over Colchester. After beating Cinderford in the next round would come a trip to Aston Villa.

Right: Two great stalwarts of the club: long-time chairman Lionel Ball and long-time Supporters' Association chairman Mick Baines at the annual cricket match between the club and supporters in 1991.

Below: Lee Turner is under pressure from the Stevenage forwards as Fleet lose out 5–1 in the FA Cup fourth qualifying round of 1996/97. Lee was made the scapegoat, despite having kept more clean sheets than any other goalkeeper, and new manager Steve Lovell allowed him to move to Margate.

Ready for the match of their lives! Players line up before taking on Aston Villa on 6 January 1996. Back row, left to right: Dean Harpley, Dave Walker, John Glover, Lee Turner, Colin Blewden, Mark Munday, Micky Cotter, Chris Weller (manager), Matt Gubbins, Mark Leahy, Mick Ward (physio). Front row: Jimmy Jackson, Paul Wilson, Ian Gibbs, Dave Powell, Grant Best, Clint Gooding, Peter Mortley.

Warm-up time and a soaking up of the atmosphere at one of the great grounds of British football – Villa Park – with players, supporters and officials all pinching themselves to realise they were playing at such a famous ground.

Fleet manager salutes his FA Cup hero

Dave Powell and Chris Weller. Dave was the top scorer in the whole of the 1995/96 FA Cup competition with 9 goals and during a five-year spell after joining from Sheppey in 1995, scored 60 goals in 225 games. Chris was assistant manager to Gary Aldous and when the latter was sacked in 1995 he stepped up and was at the helm for the cup run before he too was fired in 1996.

Jimmy Bullard (1978–). Born in East Ham, Bullard made an instant impression on joining from Dartford and won the player of the month award in August 1998 (pictured), his first month with the club. He was sold to West Ham for £35,000 the following February and later played for Peterborough, Wigan, Fulham, Hull and Ipswich and was a member of several England squads without actually being capped.

Roy Hodgson (1947–). Born in Croydon, Hodgson, along with Jimmy Bullard, is Fleet's most famous ex-player. He helped the side to promotion to the Southern League Premier Division during his two-year spell between 1969 and 1971, making 59 appearances and scoring once as a midfielder. He is much better known for his coaching and managerial abilities that have taken him all over the world and more recently to the helm at Fulham, Liverpool and West Brom.

9

BACK TO THE
CONFERENCE
2000–6

Minehead-born Andy Ford (1954–) began with his home-town team before moving into the Football League with Bournemouth, Swindon, Southend and Gillingham at full-back. Despite having only limited managerial experience, he was appointed Gravesend manager in 1997 and after a rocky start became the club's longest-serving manager (1997–2005) and, perhaps more importantly, the most successful, winning five trophies.

Jimmy Jackson proudly holds his England shirt up after becoming the first player from the Fleet to earn such an honour (playing for England non-League) and in 2005 reached another milestone by breaking Ken Burrett's long-standing appearance record. The Gravesend-born-and-bred player had played for the club since 1994 apart from one season at Dagenham, but remained part-time to help with the family farm just outside of town in Cobham. He left the Fleet in 2006 when the club required that all players be full-time.

The programme from the Gravesend v Folkestone Kent Senior Cup final of 2000. Fleet would go on to beat Dover 4–0 in the following season's final and Margate 5–0 in 2002 to complete a spectacular hat-trick of cup successes.

THE KENT COUNTY FOOTBALL ASSOCIATION
KENT SENIOR CUP FINAL
at
Stonebridge Road, Northfleet

1889   2000

FOLKESTONE INVICTA
-v-
GRAVESEND & NORTHFLEET F.C.

MONDAY 1st May 2000
KICK OFF 3.00 p.m.
Souvenir Programme £2.00

FOLKESTONE INVICTA

Colours: Black & Amber striped shirts.
Black shorts, Amber Socks

1. DAVE WIETECHA
2. ANDY MORRIS
3. IAN HAYES
4. ANDY LARKIN
5. LEE PALMER
6. BILLY MANUEL
7. CARLTON WYNTER
8. PAUL CHAMBERS
9. STEVE LAWRENCE
10. NICKY DENT
11. JEFF ROSS
12. BRETT SMITH
14. JAMES DRYDEN
15. JOHN AYLING

Manager: Mr N Cugley

Todays Ball Sponsor is
Apex Computer & Stationery Supplies Ltd.

GRAVESEND & NORTHFLEET

Colours: Red shirts, White shorts, Red socks

1. DARREN SMITH
2. MATT LEE
3. JIMMY JACKSON
4. DARREN GOWLER
5. CORY CAMPBELL
6. CRAIG WILKINS
7. STEVE RESTARICK
8. LEE SPILLER
9. DAVE POWELL
10. CHE STADHART
11. NICK HEGLEY
12. JONATHON DIFFORD
14. KIRK DODGSON
15. DREW WATKINS

Manager: Mr A Ford

REFEREE   M S Yerby   Assistant Referees F Mead   J Wills   Fourth Official   D Buck
EXTRA TIME - If the scores are level after ninety minutes, then extra time (two 15 minute periods) will be played. If the scores remain level the match will be decided by kicks from the penalty mark.

PRESENTATION - The presentation of the Cup and awards will be made by Mr Barry Bright

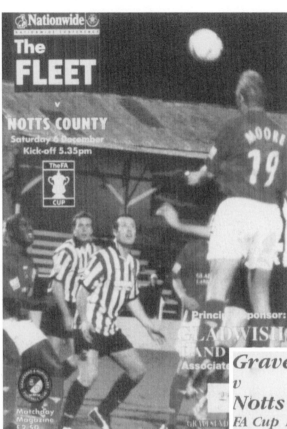

The win over Chester City in the first round of the FA Cup provided another joust at Notts County in the second round, this time in front of a national live audience on Sky television, but alas the result was a repeat of the 2000 game – a narrow 2–1 win for County.

The new century provided a good start to the club's FA Cup ambitions with several good performances. The match against Notts County, featuring top scorer Che Stadhart on the cover, had to be moved to Gillingham because of constant waterlogging of the Stonebridge Road pitch.

Charlie MacDonald was comfortably top scorer in 2005/06 despite an injury-hit season. He made a handful of Premiership appearances for Charlton in 2001.

Charlie MacDonald might be on his knees but he has just scored the only goal of the game to see off high-flyers Morecambe in 2005.

Conference here we come! After a 21-year exile, Fleet were back where they belong as Che Stadhart (far right) fires home in the 1–0 win at Bedford in the final league game of the 2001/2 campaign.

Celebration time as Jimmy Jackson lifts the Ryman Isthmian League championship.

The FA Cup brought little luck in a series of games against Football League sides, none more so than the trip to Huddersfield in the 2001/2 competition. Everything started well with Fleet taking a second-minute lead when Jamie Clarke headed Eliot Martin's teasing corner into his own net.

Fleet held the lead for more than an hour before conceding the equaliser and then after seemingly endless injury time, Leon Knight scored a memorable winning goal with a long-distance shot that Jamie Turner tries desperately to save while Jamie Vincent gets ready to celebrate.

Roy Essandoh (1976–). Born in Belfast of Ghanaian descent, 'much travelled' is an understatement for Essandoh, with his famously brief stint at Wycombe helping them into an FA Cup semi-final by heading the winning goal against Premier League Leicester in 2001. In his spell at Stonebridge Road in 2004/5 he scored 19 goals in 50 appearances before moving on to Kettering.

Andy Drury (1983–). Born in Minster, Drury joined his local club Sittingbourne before moving to Fleet in 2003 where he soon became an influential midfielder. He made 101 appearances and scored 19 goals before leaving for Lewes in 2006 deciding to remain part-time when Fleet opted to go full-time. He later moved to Stevenage, Luton and then on to Ipswich for £150,000 in 2011. He is pictured on the right.

Nick Burton played for Fleet between 2001 and 2003 and was an integral part of the team that was promoted and then consolidated itself in the Conference. In 67 games he scored 3 goals.

Matt Lee, another member of the team to win promotion and then consolidate in the Conference. Between 1999 and 2004 he played 168 times for the Fleet.

Lee Shearer (1977–). Born in Southend, Shearer was a regular during 2003/4 as Fleet consolidated their position in the Conference. He normally played in central defence, but scored once in 34 games. It was a special one, too – he headed past debutant Shrewsbury goalkeeper, sixteen-year-old Joe Hart, in a 1–1 draw.

Sponsorship at non-league level is a vital method of keeping the wolf from the door and for 2006/7 Fleet managed to obtain a deal with Austrian Airlines. Fleet players Charlie MacDonald, Ross Smith and Mark DeBolla show off the away kit with airline officials. The following year an even bigger coup was announced with Eurostar which ran between 2007 and 2011.

10

SUCCESS AT WEMBLEY AND THE MYFC YEARS 2007–12

Fleet line up proudly at Wembley in front of their fans. From the left are Moore, Long, Bostwick, Hawkins, Barrett, Akinde, Smith, Opinel, McPhee, Cronin, McCarthy and Daish.

The club has had five chairman during the new century, clockwise from the top in order of taking on the role are Brian Kilcullen (2000–6) and again temporarily in 2008, Jason Botley 2006–8, John Moules (2008–9), Duncan Holt (2009–10) and Phil Sonsara (2010–).

Lee Shearer challenges the Hereford defence in one of the last games played in front of the Northfleet terraces – soon to be declared unsafe and closed down during the 2004/5 season.

Roy Essandoh shows his strength in the air to score against Tamworth later in the same season but where are the crowd? They were actually banned from the crumbling terraces until seating was installed during the 2006/7 season.

EBBSFLEET UNITED V TORQUAY UNITED

10 MAY 2008

ENTRANCES OPEN 12:30
KICK OFF 14:30

ENTRANCE K

BLOCK 546

ROW 10

SEAT 199

25.00

THE FA CARLSBERG TROPHY FINAL

EBBSFLEET UNITED

WEMBLEY STADIUM

9346206233

THE FINAL

EBBSFLEET UNITED v TORQUAY UNITED

THE FA CARLSBERG TROPHY FINAL 2008
WEMBLEY STADIUM, SATURDAY 10 MAY 2008, KICK-OFF 2.30PM

TheFA.com

The programme and ticket from Fleet's great day.

EBBSFLEET UNITED
HOW THEY GOT HERE

FIRST ROUND PROPER:
Ebbsfleet United 4-1 Carshalton Athletic

The Fleet were made to work hard by a dogged Carshalton side, but Chris McPhee slotted home on 14 minutes to settle the nerves. The visitors drew level on 33 minutes and arguably had the better chances up to the break. McPhee's second goal six minutes into the second half seemed to knock the stuffing out of the Surrey team and Fleet stamped their authority on the game after that. Luke Moore scored with a lofted shot on 77 minutes and John Akinde rubbed salt into the Robins' wound by stabbing home from close range to make it 4-1.

SECOND ROUND PROPER:
Dorchester Town 0-2 Ebbsfleet United

The Fleet travelled down to Dorset in the next round, facing the team that had just knocked out the holders Stevenage Borough. The Conference South outfit were looking for a second upset, but it wasn't to be. Midfielder Neil Barrett played in Akinde on 16 minutes and the teenager rounded the 'keeper to slide the ball into the net. Dorchester didn't record a shot on target until the 35th minute and the second half got off to the worse possible start for the hosts as Akinde picked out McPhee after two minutes and he fired home from 12 yards.

THIRD ROUND PROPER:
Ebbsfleet United 1-0 Weymouth

The Fleet's progress into the last eight was sealed by a Neil Barrett goal midway through the second half of this all-Conference Premier clash at Stonebridge Road. The opening 20 minutes were cagey, with chances at a premium. The home side came out for the second half looking purposeful, but James Smith headed just over from a good position. With Purcell and Eribenne about to enter the fray, Fleet got the breakthrough goal as Barrett saw his initial shot parried by the 'keeper but pounced on the rebound to slam the ball high into the net.

FOURTH ROUND PROPER:
Burton Albion 0-0 Ebbsfleet United
Replay: Ebbsfleet United 1-0 Burton Albion

The Fleet's quarter final took them to Pirelli Stadium and it was Burton who started the stronger. The second half was more open than the first, with neither side wanting a replay. A superb block by Peter Hawkins denied Burton's Gilroy and Moore's late effort almost put the visitors through at the first attempt. Fleet took a while to get going in their home replay three days later and often found Burton content to sit deep in their own half. The tie went to extra time, Stacy Long finally forcing in the winner to send Stonebridge Road into pandemonium.

SEMI-FINAL FIRST LEG:
Ebbsfleet United 3-1 Aldershot Town

SEMI-FINAL SECOND LEG:
Aldershot Town 1-1 Ebbsfleet United

Liam Daish's "Believe" mentality showed through as the Fleet set about Conference Premier leaders Aldershot with intent from the first whistle. Chukki Eribenne was tripped on six minutes and McPhee stepped up to drill home the first of two successful spot-kicks. The Shots hit back with a goal on 76 minutes before Paul McCarthy prodded in a third for the hosts. Fleet launched themselves into the second leg, growing in confidence after a goalless first half. Shots scored as the rain lashed down, but Michael Bostwick then carved his name in history by making it 1-1 on the day in injury time.

Lance Cronin made 199 appearances for Fleet between 2006 and 2010 and made no more important save than this one at Wembley early on when Fleet were still settling down after Torquay's bright start.

The drama unfolds as Luke Moore is upended by Torquay goalkeeper Simon Rayner. Penalty!

Chris McPhee shapes up to shoot . . .

. . . but his shot is saved by Rayner leaving McPhee in despair; John Akinde cant believe it either.

What a difference a minute makes as McPhee forgets his woe to stroke home John Akinde's pass and Michael Bostwick closes in to give him a kiss!

Chris McPhee salutes his unwell sister with his '4 U SIS' shirt.

Fleet celebrate a hard-earned victory.

Captain Paul McCarthy and manager Liam
Daish celebrate a job well done.

The club were granted a civic reception to celebrate the FA Trophy success and crowd favourite Sacha Opinel has just shown the crowd the trophy.

Luke Moore (1988–). Born in Gravesend, Moore was one of the first of the PASE youth scheme to come through. After 109 games and 20 goals he left for AFC Wimbledon helping them to successfully gain a place in the Football League.

Sacha Opinel and Michael Bostwick sandwich a Weymouth player on the way to FA Trophy glory. Both played a key role in the success with Bostwick going on to win again the following season in a Stevenage shirt along with Stacy Long.

Stacy Long (1985–). Born in Bromley, Long started at Charlton before moving to Notts County. He signed for Fleet in 2006 leaving in 2009 for Stevenage after 117 games and 18 goals.

Neil Barrett (1981–). Born in Tooting, midfielder Barrett started at Chelsea before moving to Scotland. He returned south to Woking before joining Fleet in 2007. Another key member of the FA Trophy success, he broke his jaw when Fleet lost out to Stevenage in the following season's trophy semi-final and that sadly proved to be his last game for the club in that spell. Barrett returned to the club in November 2011 after spells at Woking and Havant.

Paul McCarthy (1971–). Born in Cork, McCarthy's long career included stints with Brighton and Wycombe as well as earning 10 caps for Ireland. He signed for Fleet in 2004 playing 136 games and scoring 6 goals as he gradually wound down his career after skippering the club at Wembley and eventually took over as assistant manager.

Michael Gash signed in 2008 from Cambridge City and top scored with a relatively modest 11-goal tally. In a vote by myfc members, an offer of £55,000 was accepted for him from York after a single season at Stonebridge Road.

Darius Charles (1987–). Born in Ealing, Charles signed from Brentford after coming originally on loan in 2008/9. He was signed for £15,000 following a myfc vote and was later sold after another vote, becoming the first player to be both bought and sold by myfc in a membership vote. He had earlier been part of an intended double sale to York with Michael Gash but decided to stay in the south for family reasons. He played 85 times for Ebbsfleet and earned 2 England non-league caps before moving to Stevenage and gaining promotion to League Division One as part of an ex-Fleet trio with Stacy Long and Michael Bostwick.

John Akinde (1989–). Born in Gravesend, Akinde was another local lad who came through the PASE scheme and after going on loan to Whitstable, came back and quickly made an impact playing a major role in the Fleet's FA Trophy triumph by laying on the only goal with his non-stop bustling. He played just 28 games for Fleet scoring 10 goals before Bristol City beat a host of clubs for his signature in exchange for £130,000 – a deal that had to be approved by a members' vote of myfc. Although the move was not a success he continued in the Football League playing for Wycombe, Bristol Rovers, Brentford and latterly Crawley.

Liam Daish (1968–). Born in Portsmouth, Daish became the club's twenty-seventh manager in February 2005. He earned a reputation as a no-nonsense defender with Portsmouth, Cambridge United, Birmingham and Coventry before injury brought an early end to his playing career. He gained managerial experience at Havant & Waterlooville and Welling before landing the Fleet job where he has had considerable success.

After years of playing on mudheaps following the building of a small industrial estate next to the ground, the club decided to invest in an expensive but necessary new drainage system in 2001 that has proved a great success. helped by the expertise of groundsman Peter Norton.

Having lost nearly all their players at the end of 2008/9 because they were out of contract, the 2009/10 season was always going to be a testing one. After winning just one league game going into December a valiant fight against relegation almost succeeded and would have but for the withdrawal of Chester two-thirds of the way through the season. A great 3–2 win at Luton was a feature as Lance Cronin defies the Luton forwards in a packed goalmouth.

Liam Hatch (1982–). Born in Hitchin, Hatch signed from Herne Bay. He then had two good seasons at Stonebridge Road between 2001 and 2003, playing 47 times and scoring 12 goals. Among his goals were several important ones in our Ryman promotion year and our first season back in the Conference, notably the winning goal against Halifax to ensure no relegation in our first year back in the top level of non-league football. Here he is pictured beating Leon Crooks to the ball and firing Luton into the lead at Kenilworth Road before Fleet hit back to win 3–2. He is currently at Darlington after an extensive Football League career with Barnet and Peterborough.

Magno Vieira (1985–). Hailing from Brasilia, Vieira is another striker to do well for Fleet, scoring 16 goals in 41 outings in our relegation year of 2009/10. Here he carries the ball back to the centre circle after scoring in the thrilling 4–3 win over Forest Green Rovers in January 2010.

Stefan Bailey miskicks as Darius Charles looks on in the 2–0 victory over Gateshead in April 2010. Sadly the victory was not quite enough to avoid relegation.

The first league meeting with old rivals Dartford in 19 seasons drew a big crowd to Princes Park as 2,781 saw a 1–1 draw in August 2010. Preston Edwards proved an effective goalkeeper filling the formidable boots of Lance Cronin and by the end of the season had gained an England non-league cap. Here he beats a Dartford forward to a cross.

Callum Willock (1981–). Born in Lambeth, experienced forward Willock, formerly with Peterborough, Port Vale and Stevenage, proved invaluable in Fleet's promotion push scoring 20 goals in 43 games, finishing top scorer in his first season with the Fleet. Young prospect Scott Ginty watches and learns in the background in the game against Maidenhead.

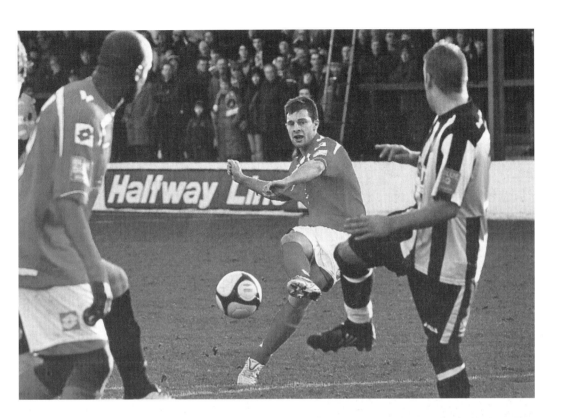

The continued success of Fleet's youth scheme saw the successors to Luke Moore and John Akinde come through in the form of Michael West (above) and Tom Phipp (right) who both played prominent parts in the promotion success.

Ricky Shakes (out of the picture) scores Fleet's third goal to seemingly secure victory over Farnborough in the Blue Square South play-off, but Boro' hit back to make it 3–2. Thankfully a last-minute goal ensured a 4–2 victory in front of a 4,000-plus crowd of which more than half had travelled down to Hampshire to support Ebbsfleet.

It's in the bag, Fleet celebrate a Michael West goal in the play-off final at Farnborough. Tom Phipp, Ram Marwa (8) and Calum Willock help him celebrate while on the left former Fleet man and member of the FA Trophy winning team of 2008 James Smith looks glum.

Fleet captain Paul Lorraine, who had been immense throughout the season in the centre of defence, holds the play-off trophy up in triumph at Farnborough after the memorable 4–2 victory.

ACKNOWLEDGEMENTS

While most of this work comes from my own collection it would have been impossible to produce this book without the valuable help of photos from Richard Ralph and Keith Chase while John Jones and Andy Porter were a great help on the Northfleet United section. The *Gravesend Reporter* and *Kent Messenger* have also always been very helpful as has Gravesend Library and the National Football Museum while photos from the 1980s come courtesy of former club photographer David Hills.